GO...
TREASURY

First published 1989 by
Poolbeg Press Ltd.
Knocksedan House,
Swords, Co. Dublin, Ireland.

© Sean McMahon 1989
Selection and Introduction

ISBN 1 85371 008 3

Cover design by Steven Hope
Typeset by Print-Forme,
62 Santry Close, Dublin 9.
Printed by The Guernsey Press Ltd.,
Vale, Guernsey, Channel Islands.

THE POOLBEG
GOLDEN TREASURY
OF WELL LOVED POEMS
EDITED BY
SEAN McMAHON

Sean McMahon, distinguished critic, anthologist and editor, lives in Derry. Among the works he has compiled and edited are:

The Best from the Bell (O'Brien Press, 1978)

A Book of Irish Quotations (O'Brien Press, 1984)

Rich and Rare: A Book of Ireland (Poolbeg, 1984)

The Poolbeg Book of Children's Verse (1987)

My Native Land: A Celebration of Britain (Poolbeg, 1987)

Fair City: A Thousand Years of Dublin (Poolbeg, 1988)

For Margaret Daly

Acknowledgements

For kind permission to reprint copyright material, the publishers gratefully acknowledge the following:

Mr R Dardis Clarke for "The Planter's Daughter" by Austin Clarke; Jonathan Cape Limited on behalf of the executors of the W. H. Davies estate for "Leisure" by W. H. Davies; Jonathan Cape Limited on behalf of the estate of Robert Frost for "The Road not Taken" by Robert Frost; Mrs Katherine B. Kavanagh c/o Peter Fallon, Loughcrew, Oldcastle, Co. Meath for "Shancoduff" and "Raglan Road" by Patrick Kavanagh; The Society of Authors as the literary representative of the estate of John Masefield for "Cargoes" by John Masefield; the estate of Enid Starkey for "A Piper" by Seumas O'Sullivan; James MacGibbon, executor of the estate of Stevie Smith for "Not Waving but Drowning" from *The Collected Poems of Stevie Smith* (Penguin Modern Classics); A. P. Watt Limited on behalf of Michael B. Yeats and Macmillan London Limited for "The Lake Isle of Innisfree," and "The Second Coming" from *The Collected Poems of W B Yeats*.

Poolbeg Press apologise for any errors or omissions in the above list and would be grateful to be notified of any corrections that should be incorporated in future editions of this book.

Contents

Introduction

It is a stiff-lipped cliché that all those hardy mountaineers climbed the Matterhorn. Kilmanjaro and Everest because they "were there." Why, in an age when, though much poetry is published, fewer people read it, should one purchase a *Golden Treasury of Well-Loved Poems*? Precisely because the poems are there. Modern poetry has drifted a little bit away from the literate person-in-the-street but he needs his poetic sustenance as much as ever. One senses that less poetry is learned by heart these days, it is claimed for good educational reasons, but the *individu moyen littéraire* who used to be his own walking anthology now feels the lack. When Humpty-Dumpty in *Through the Looking-Glass* said "There's glory for you," he wasn't actually referring to the accumulated treasury of accessible poetry but he might well have been. This book is a tap-root to that well, to change the metaphor without too much forcing.

In my boyhood I met people who had had no access to education beyond the national school who could recite Grey's "Elegy" without falter and give "I am Monarch of All I Survey" as an encore. They could also do selected speeches from Shakespeare and bits from Davis, Mangan and Kipling. Their repertoire may have been their only experience of poetry (which they regularly added to) and those who did "All the World's a Stage" probably had not read let alone seen *As You Like It*. For most of them *The Deserted Village* consisted of the portraits of schoolmaster and parson with most of the poem unread. Yet not even the daftest educational theorist (than which few species are dafter) will argue that some poetry is worse than no poetry and if they further say that poetry should not be spoken or read aloud then the declamatory ghost of Yeats will rise and intone some sense into them. The greater number of the poems in this collection belong to a period of poetic accessibility and that basis of choice should also be the basis of judgement.

What does this poetry do for people? It may in Auden's words make nothing happen yet it does have an appeal. It may answer a need; it may put into words some half-formed thought; it may startle into some simple insight; it may have the satisfying effect of a good aphorism—in Pope's words, "What oft was thought, but ne'er so well expressed." It may even be anodyne, like a mild sedative. Such lines as "Here at the quiet limit of the world" are quite tranquillising. I think that the detractors of such verse would be hard put to prove it harmful. People respond to rhythm; if they idly tap their fingers on a table they soon devise a beat. People given half a chance would become poets again and in the older days the good ones were rightly prized.

This collection should offend only by its exclusions, as Francis Turner Palgrave who invented the term, Golden Treasury wrote in his introduction to the first edition, a hundred and thirty-eight years ago, "The editor will regard as his fittest readers those who love poetry so well that he can offer them nothing not already known and valued." 'Tis but a little volume and selection has been a sore trial. Certain poets, Shakespeare, Milton, Burns, Wordsworth and many more including Yeats demand anthologies of their own. Some others hold their place by reason of one happy success. Yet one good poem is enough for a stand-seat on Parnassus. Those who may with justice complain that their particular favourite is not included will, however, know where that favourite may be found. My hope, indeed my expectation, is that wherever the reader may open this book what he finds will be to his taste, may answer some need, may give a moment of wisely unanalysed pleasure. The apparent immediacy of meaning does not daunt as some stuff "all out of shape from toe to top" and often they will reveal subtleties that casual reading cannot discover. The age of public poetry may be over but these survivals are worth their room.

I should like to take this opportunity to thank my editor, Jo O'Donoghue for firm kindness and help.

Sean McMahon
1989

My Lady Greensleeves

Anonymous (16th Century)

"Greensleeves" was published in 1581. The well-known air is sometimes attributed to Henry VIII and it was used for other contemporary ballads. Shakespeare mentions it twice in *The Merry Wives of Windsor* and it was used as a rallying cry for the Cavalier party during the English Civil War. The green that the inconstant lady wore may have indicated her oldest profession.

Alas! my love, you do me wrong
    To cast me off discourteously;
And I have loved you so long,
    Delighting in your company.

Greensleeves was all my joy!
Greensleeves was my delight!
Greensleeves was my heart of gold!
    And who but my Lady Greensleeves!

I bought thee petticoats of the best,
    The cloth so fine as fine as might be;
I gave thee jewels for thy chest,
    And all this cost I spent on thee.
        Greensleeves, etc.

Thy smock of silk, both fair and white,
    With gold embroidered gorgeously;
Thy petticoat of sendal right:
    And these I bought thee gladly.
        Greensleeves, etc.

Thy gown was of the grassy green,
 The sleeves of satin hanging by;
Which made thee be our harvest queen:
 And yet thou wouldest not love me!
  Greensleeves, etc.

Greensleeves now farewell! adieu!
 God I pray to prosper thee!
For I am still thy lover true:
 Come once again and love me!

Greensleeves was all my joy!
 Greensleeves was my delight!
Greensleeves was my heart of gold!
 And who but my Lady Greensleeves

The Passionate Shepherd to His Love

Christopher Marlowe

Kit Marlowe was born in Canterbury in 1564, a few months before his greater rival, Shakespeare. He was sent by his father, a prosperous shoemaker, to Corpus Christi Cambridge. Between 1587 and 1593 he had presented seven tragedies including *Dr Faustus, Tamburlaine* and *The Jew of Malta*. His private life was stormy: he was an avowed atheist, may have been a Catholic and was probably a secret agent. His death at Deptford on 1 June 1593 at the hand of Ingram Frizer which was given out as part of a tavern brawl may have been political. At his death his work was preferred to Shakespeare's.

"Come live with me" was a typical pastoral of the period in spite of the unidyllic English weather; Marlowe is apostrophied as "dead shepherd" in *As You Like It..*

Come live with me, and be my love,
And we will all the pleasures prove
That valleys, groves, hills and field,
Woods, or steepy mountain yields.

And we will sit upon the rocks,
Seeing the shepherds feed their flocks
By shallow rivers, to whose falls
Melodious birds sing madrigals.

And I will make thee beds of roses
And a thousand fragrant posies,
A cap of flowers, and a kirtle
Embroidered all with leaves of myrtle.

A gown made of the finest wool
Which from our pretty lambs we pull,
Fair lined slippers for the cold
With buckles of the purest gold.

A belt of straw and ivy buds
With coral clasps and amber studs;
And if these pleasures may thee move,
Come live with me, and be my love.

The shepherd swains shall dance and sing
For thy delight each May-morning.
If these delights thy mind may move,
Then live with me, and be my love.

All the World's a Stage

William Shakespeare

William Shakespeare was born on 23 April 1564 and died on the same date in 1616. His is buried beneath the chancel of Holy Trinity Church in Stratford-u-Avon and the heroic exactness of the number of his years is only one of many myths associated with this greatest English writer. His father, John, was a leather bleacher, born in Snitterfield, who after marriage to Mary Arden of Wilmcote settled down in the prosperous market town of Stratford. He married Anne Hathaway of Shottery, another village in Stratford's purlieu and had three children by her, one of which, Hamnet a twin, and his only son, died young. By 1592 he was one of the playwrights and actors in the theatre-mad London of Elizabeth I. He wrote at least 34 plays which are so sympathetic to the thoughts and feelings of men and written in language so memorable that they supply slogans for all factions. Shakespeare the man, remains elusive: as Matthew Arnold puts it.

Others abide our question; thou art free.

One of many poetic speeches that makes Shakespeare a "Golden Treasury" on his own. It is spoken by the cynical, diseased Jaques in *As You Like It* and is complimentary to none of the ages. "Totus mundus agit historionem," Petronius's version of the first line was the motto of Shakespeare's own theatre on the South Bank, the "great Globe itself."

All the world's a stage,
And all the men and women merely players:
They have their exits and their entrance;
And one man in his time plays many parts,
His acts being seven ages. At first the infant,
Mewling and puking in the nurse's arms.
And then the whining schoolboy, with his satchel,
And shining morning face, creeping like snail
Unwillingly to school. And then the lover,
Sighing like furnace, with a woeful ballad
Made to his mistress' eyebrow. Then a soldier,
Full of strange oaths, and bearded like the pard,
Jealous in honour, sudden and quick in quarrel,
Seeking the bubble reputation
Even in the cannon's mouth. And then the justice,
In fair round belly with good capon lined,
With eyes severe and beard of formal cut,
Full of wise saws and modern instances;
And so he plays his part. The sixth age shifts
Into the lean and slippered pantaloon,
With spectacles on nose, and pouch on side;
His youthful hose, well saved, a world too wide
For his shrunk shank; and his big manly voice,
Turning again toward childish treble, pipes
And whistles in his sound. Last scene of all,
That ends this strange eventful history,
Is second childishness and mere oblivion,
Sans teeth, sans eyes, sans taste, sans everything.

from Fear No More The Heat O' The Sun

William Shakespeare

This most beautiful of threnodies comes from *Cymbeline*, a crazily variegated Romance. It is spoken by Guiderius and Arviragus over the dead body of their friend, Fidele. They think they are called Polydore and Cadwal and that their father is Morgan. What they do not know is that Fidele is really their sister, Imogen, and that their father is Cymbeline, and that she is not dead at all. It is a case of "lovely lament, shame about the plot."

> Fear no more the heat o' the sun,
>   Nor the furious winter's rages;
> Thou thy worldly task hast done,
>   Home art gone, and ta'en thy wages:
> Golden lads and girls all must,
> As chimney-sweepers, come to dust.
>
> Fear no more the frown o' the great,
>   Thou are past the tyrant's stroke;
> Care no more to clothe and eat;
>   To thee the reed is as the oak:
> The sceptre, learning, physic, must
> All follow this, and come to dust.
>
> Fear no more the lightning-flash
>   Nor the all-dreaded thunder-stone;
> Fear not slander, censure rash;
>   Thou has finish'd joy and moan:
> All lovers young, all lovers must
> Consign to thee, and come to dust.

In Plague Time

Thomas Nashe

Thomas Nash(e) was born in 1567 in Lowestoft, the son of a clergyman, and educated at St John's College, Cambridge. He was an active and effective pamphleteer by 1588 and was leading a turbulent life, which included a prison sentence and much public anti-Puritan rhetoric.

The thoughts of this poem are nothing if not sententious but it has great dramatic dignity and sung as a threnody, as in a recent Stratford production of *Romeo and Juliet*, is most moving. It comes from a play called *Summer's Last Will and Testament*, written just before Nash died in 1601.

Adieu, farewell earth's bliss,
This world uncertain is;
Fond are life's lustful joys,
Death proves them all but toys,
None from his darts can fly.
I am sick, I must die.
       Lord, have mercy on us!

Rich men, trust not in wealth,
Gold cannot buy you health;
Physic himself must fade,
All things to end are made.
The plague full swift goes by.
I am sick, I must die.
       Lord, have mercy on us!

Beauty is but a flower
Which wrinkles will devour;
Brightness falls from the air,
Queens have died young and fair,
Dust hath closed Helen's eye.
I am sick, I must die.
        Lord have mercy on us!

Strength stoops unto the grave,
Worms feed on Hector brave,
Swords may not fight with fate,
Earth still holds ope her gate.
Come! come! the bells do cry.
I am sick, I must die.
        Lord, have mercy on us!

Wit with his wantonness
Tasteth death's bitterness;
Hell's executioner
Hath no ears for to hear
What vain art can reply.
I am sick, I must die.
        Lord, have mercy on us!

Haste, therefore, each degree,
To welcome destiny.
Heaven is our heritage,
Earth but a player's stage;
Mount we unto the sky.
I am sick, I must die.
        Lord, have mercy on us!

Song

John Donne

John Donne was born in London in 1572 and brought up as a Catholic, a faith he relinquished in his twenties. He married Ann More in 1601, a move which caused him public disgrace and the forfeiture of a career in the public service. He eventually took orders and by 1621 had sufficiently been restored to royal favour to be appointed Dean of St Paul's. His sermons were famous in his time, obscuring the excellence of his often difficult poetry. His complicated imagination and poetic skill makes him the foremost of the "metaphysicals." Much obsessed by death and resurrection he had his portrait painted in his shroud and standing upon a funeral urn, as he would look on Doomsday. He died the father of twelve children in 1631, having been predeceased by his wife fourteen years.

> Goe, and catche a falling starre,
>   Get with child a mandrake roote,
> Tell me, where all past years are,
>   Or who cleft the Divels foot,
> Teach me to heare Mermaids singing,
> Or to keep off envies stinging,
>   And finde
>   What winde
> Serves to advance an honest minde.
>
> If thou beest borne to strange sights,
>   Things invisible to see,
> Ride ten thousand daies and nights,

Till age snow white haires on thee,
Thou, when thou retorn'st, wilt tell mee
All strange wonders that befell thee,
      And sweare
      No where
Lives a woman true, and faire.

If thous findst one, let mee know,
     Such a Pilgrimage were sweet;
Yet doe not, I would not goe,
     Though at next doore wee might meet,
Though shee were true, when you met her,
And last, till you write your letter,
      Yet shee
      Will bee
False, ere I come, to two, or three.

The Canonization

John Donne

For Godsake hold your tongue, and let me love,
   Or chide my palsie, or my gout,
My five gray hairs, or ruin'd fortune flout,
    With wealth your state, your minde with Arts improve,
     Take you a course, get you a place,
     Observe his honour, or his grace,
Or the Kings reall, or his stamped face,
    Contemplate, what you will, approve,
    So you will let me love.

Alas, alas, who's injur'd by my love?
   What merchants ships have my sighs drown'd?
Who saies my teares have overflow'd his ground?
    When did my colds a forward spring remove?
     When did the heats which my veins fill
     Adde one man to the plaguie Bill?
Soldiers finde warres, and Lawyers finde out still
    Litigious men, which quarrels move,
    Though she and I do love.

Call us what you will, wee are made such by love;
   Call her one, mee another flye,
We'are Tapers too, and at our owne cost die,
    And wee in us finde the 'Eagle and the Dove.
     The Pheonix ridle hath more wit
     By us, we two being one, are it.
So to one neutrall thing both sexes fit,
    Wee dye and rise the same, and prove
    Mysterious by this love.

Wee can dye by it, if not live by love,
 And if unfit from tombes and hearse
Our legend bee, it will be fit for verse;
 And if no peece of Chronicle wee prove,
  We'll build on sonnets pretty roomes;
  As well a well wrought urne becomes
The greatest ashes, as halfe-acre tombes,
 And by these hymns, all shall approve
 Us *Canoniz'd* for Love:

And thus invoke us; You whom reverend love
 Made one anothers hermitage;
You, to whom love was peace, that now is rage;
 Who did the whole worlds soule contract, and drove
  Into the glasses of your eyes
  (So made such mirrors, and such spies,
That they did all to you epitomize,)
 Countries, Townes, Court: Beg from above
 A patterne of your love!

To Celia

Ben Jonson

Ben Jonson was born in Westminster, the posthumous son of a Border clergyman, in 1572. He led a stormy life including the known killing of several men, among them Gabriel Spence, a fellow actor, in a duel, being arrested for sedition, becoming a Catholic and later relinquishing that faith, and eventually as a quarrelsome deviser of masques at the court of James 1. His best plays, *Volpone* (1601), *The Alchemist* (1610) and *Bartholomew Fair* (1614) are still performed. He died in 1637. The thoughts in this famous song lyric were suggested by the prose of Philostratos, the 4th-century B.C. Greek writer.

Drink to me only with thine eyes,
    And I will pledge with mine;
Or leave a kiss but in the cup
    And I'll not look for wine.
The thirst that from the soul doth rise
    Doth ask a drink divine;
But might I of Jove's nectar sup,
    I would not change for thine.

I sent thee late a rosy wreath,
    Not so much honouring thee
As giving it a hope that there
    It could not wither'd be;
But thou thereon didst only breathe,
    And sent'st it back to me;
Since when it grows and smells, I swear,
    Not of itself but thee!

Golden Slumbers

Thomas Dekker

Thomas Dekker was born about 1572, one of the few native Londoners who became famous as playwrights to have been born in the city. He was frequently in debt and was imprisoned for it at least once but it does not seem to have affected his kindly sunny nature. He was a famous pamphleteer: his *Gull's Handbook* (1609) still makes jolly reading. He collaborated with Ford, Rowley, Middleton and Webster but his most famous play, *The Shoemaker's Holiday* (1600) is his own work. Charles Lamb said, "He has poetry enough for anything," as this famous lullaby shows. It comes from his play *Patient Grissel* (1603) about the Decameron Doormat. He died about 1632.

> Golden slumbers kiss your eyes,
> Smiles awake you when you rise:
> Sleep, pretty wantons, do not cry,
> And I will sing a lullaby.
> Rock them, rock them, lullaby.
>
> Care is heavy, therefore sleep you.
> You are care, and care must keep you:
> Sleep, pretty wantons, do not cry,
> And I will sing a lullaby.
> Rock them, rock them, lullaby.

Gather Ye Rose-Buds

Robert Herrick

Robert Herrick was born in 1591, the son of a London goldsmith who afterwards committed suicide. He was apprenticed to the trade but was allowed to go to St John's College, Cambridge from which he took orders and he was given the living of Dean Prior, a remote Devonshire village, in 1629. He was bitterly anti-Puritan and lost the living during the Commonwealth. He recovered it at the Restoration and died in 1674. He is one of the finest song-lyricists in English as this little piece shows and he seems to have had no difficulty in reconciling his amorism with his reverend calling, at least on paper.

> Gather ye rose-buds while ye may,
>   Old Time is still a flying:
> And this same flower that smiles to-day
>   To-morrow will be dying.
>
> The glorious lamp of heaven, the sun,
>   The higher he's a getting
> The sooner will his race be run,
>   And nearer he's to setting.
>
> That age is best which is the first,
>   When youth and blood are warmer:
> But being spent, the worse, and worst
>   Times, still succeed the former.
>
> Then be not coy, but use your time;
>   And while ye may, go marry:
> For having lost but once your prime,
>   You may for ever tarry.

Sonnet on His Blindness

John Milton

John Milton was born in 1608 in London and led a life in which Humanism and Puritanism struggled for mastery. After Shakespeare he is the most gifted English poet with much greater classical learning and performance. His epic *Paradise Lost* was written between 1658 and 1664 and *Samson Agonistes* his exact imitation of a Sophoclean tragedy in 1671. His poems "L'Allegro" and "Il Penseroso" show the Renaissance side of his character but he was a strong anti-Royalist and Cromwell's foreign secretary during the Commonwealth. He was eventually pardoned by Charles II and spent the last twelve years of his life blind but well-tended by his third wife who was forty years his junior.

When I consider how my light is spent,
    Ere half my days, in this dark world and wide,
    And that one talent which is death to hide,
    Lodg'd with me useless, though my soul more bent
To serve therewith my Maker, and present
    My true account, lest He returning chide,
    Doth God exact day-labour, light deny'd,
    I fondly ask; But patience to prevent
That murmur, soon replies, God doth not need
    Either man's work or His own gifts, who best
    Bear His mild yoke, they serve Him best, His state
Is kingly. Thousands at His bidding speed
    And post o'er Land and Ocean without rest:
    They also serve who only stand and wait.

A Constant Lover

Sir John Suckling

Sir John Suckling, born in 1609, was the copybook Cavalier poet and dramatist, rich, witty, gorgeous in attire and recklessly Royalist—all characteristics to set the rising Puritans' teeth on edge. His plays, like most Caroline pieces, are dead but he lives in many naughtily witty short poems. It is likely that it was the elegance of this little squib as much as its paper libertinism that enraged the King's enemies. A noted gambler, he is credited with the invention of the game of cribbage. He failed to rescue the King's favourite, Strafford, from the tower, and fled to the continent where he committed suicide by poison in 1642.

Out upon it, I have loved
    Three whole days together!
And am like to love three more,
    If it prove fair weather.

Time shall moult away his wings
    Ere he shall discover
In the whole wide world again
    Such a constant lover.

But the spite on 't is, no praise
    Is due at all to me:
Love with me had made no stays,
    Had it any been but she.

Had it any been but she,
    And that very face,
There had been at least ere this
    A dozen dozen in her place.

Wishes for the Supposed Mistress

Richard Crashaw

Richard Crashaw was born in 1612 or 1613 in London. Both mother and stepmother died before he was nine and his father died when he was thirteen. He went to Charterhouse and Pembroke College, Cambridge where his Puritanism gave way to High Anglicanism, and he finally became a Catholic in 1645 when it was expedient for all such to fly to the continent. After much hardship he found some appropriate work in Italy but died in 1649. His poetry is full of "conceits"—especially the religious work—but in this, his best known poem, he is witty and not at all impossible.

> Whoe'er she be,
> That not impossible She
> That shall command my heart and me;
>
> Where'er she lie,
> Lock'd up from mortal eye
> In shady leaves of destiny:
>
> Till that ripe birth
> Of studied Fate stand forth,
> And teach her fair steps to our earth;
>
> Till that divine
> Idea take a shrine
> Of crystal flesh, through which to shine:
>
> —Meet you her, my Wishes,
> Bespeak her to my blisses,
> And be ye call'd, my absent kisses.

I wish her beauty
That owes not all its duty
To gaudy tire, or glist'ring shoe-tie:

Something more than
Taffata or tissue can,
Or rampant feather, or rich fan.

A face that's best
By its own beauty drest,
And can alone command the rest:

A face made up
Out of no other shop
Than what Nature's white hand sets ope.

Sydneian showers
Of sweet discourse, whose powers
Can crown old Winter's head with flowers.

Whate'er delight
Can make day's forehead bright
Or give down to the wings of night.

Soft silken hours,
Open suns, shady bowers;
'Bove all, nothing within that lowers.

Days, that need borrow
No part of their good morrow
From a fore-spent night of sorrow:

Days, that in spite
Of darkness, by the light
Of a clear mind are day all night.

Life, that dares send
A challenge to his end,
And when it comes, say, "Welcome, friend."

I wish her store
Of worth may leave her poor
Of wishes; and I wish—no more.

—Now, if Time knows
That Her, whose radiant brows
Weave them a garland of my vows;

Her that dares be
What these lines wish to see:
I seek no further, it is She.

'Tis She, and here
Lo! I unclothe and clear
My wishes' cloudy character.

Such worth as this is
Shall fix my flying wishes,
And determine them to kisses.

Let her full glory,
My fancies, fly before ye;
Be ye my fictions:—but her story.

To Lucasta, Going to the Wars

Richard Lovelace

Richard Lovelace was born in 1618 in Woolwich, and was, like his older friend, Suckling, handsome, rich and Royalist. He was involved in anti-Parliament activity long before the Civil War. His bond of release from prison precluded further public support for the King but all his money went to the royalist cause. He died in poverty in 1657, remembered by some few poems including, "To Althea from Prison" and this famous piece written in 1645 when he left for service with Louis XIV.

Tell me not, Sweet, I am unkind,
    That from the nunnery
Of thy chaste breast, and quiet mind,
    To war and arms I fly.

True; a new mistress now I chase,
    The first foe in the field;
And with a stronger faith embrace
    A sword, a horse, a shield.

Yet this inconstancy is such
    As thou too shalt adore;
I could not love thee, Dear, so much,
    Loved I not Honour more

To His Coy Mistress

Andrew Marvell

Andrew Marvell was born in Yorkshire in 1621. Although a friend of Lovelace he was a noted but independent supporter of Cromwell and the parliament. In spite of fearless criticism of Charles II's ministers the King was fond of him, and though he succeeded Milton as Cromwell's Latin Secretary and wrote poems praising the Protector he had sufficient standing at the Restoration to arrange for Milton to be pardoned. His poetry was almost unread until mid-nineteenth century American readers "discovered" him. He is now the most popular and most enigmatic of all the metaphysicals. He died in 1678 in London as a result of medical malpractice. This is his most famous poem, witty, often quoted and yet in the penultimate image of the "ball" quite obscure.

> Had we but world enough, and time,
> This coyness, Lady, were no crime.
> We would sit down, and think which way
> To walk, and pass our long love's day.
> Thou by the Indian Ganges' side
> Shouldst rubies find: I by the tide
> Of Humber would complain. I would
> Love you ten years before the Flood:
> And you should, if you please, refuse
> Till the conversion of the Jews.
> My vegetable love should grow
> Vaster than empires, and more slow.
> An hundred years should go to praise

Thine eyes, and on thy forehead gaze.
Two hundred to adore each breast:
But thirty thousand to the rest.
An age at least to every part,
And the last age should show your heart.
For, Lady, you deserve this state;
Nor would I love at lower rate.
But at my back I always hear
Time's wingèd chariot hurrying near:
And yonder all before us lie
Deserts of vast eternity.
Thy beauty shall no more be found;
Nor, in thy marble vault, shall sound
My echoing song: then worms shall try
That long preserved virginity:
And your quaint honour turn to dust;
And into ashes all my lust.
The grave's a fine and private place,
But none I think do there embrace.
Now therefore, while the youthful hue
Sits on thy skin like morning dew,
And while thy willing soul transpires
At every pore with instant fires,
Now let us sport us while we may;
And now, like amorous birds of prey,
Rather at once our time devour,
Than languish in his slow-chapt power.
Let us roll all our strength, and all
Our sweetness, up into one ball:
And tear our pleasures with rough strife,
Thorough the iron gates of life.
Thus, though we cannot make our sun
Stand still, yet we will make him run.

Sally in Our Alley

Henry Carey

Henry Carey was born sometime in the decade before 1700 and became a characteristic journeyman of the eighteenth-century theatre. As well as this famous song he was also credited with some of the verses of "God Save the King." His satirical attack on the playwright, Ambrose Phillips, gave the word "namby-pamby" to the language. His mock of the fruity plays of the day, *Chrononhotonthologos* (1734) he described as "The Most Tragical Tragedy that was ever Tragedized by any company of Tragedians". He died in 1743. The idea for this song came as he followed behind a shoemaker's apprentice who "was making a holiday with his sweetheart, treated her with a sight of Bedlam, the puppet shows, the flying chairs, and all the elegancies of Moorfields, whence, proceeding to the Farthing Pie House, he gave her a collation of buns, cheesecakes, gammon of bacon, stuffed beer and bottled ale, through all which scenes the author dodged them."

Of all the girls that are so smart
    There's none like pretty Sally;
She is the darling of my heart,
    And she lives in our alley.
There is no lady in the land
    Is half so sweet as Sally;
She is the darling of my heart,
    And she lives in our alley.

Her father he makes cabbage-nets,
    And through the street does cry 'em;
Her mother she sells laces long
    To such as please to buy 'em:
But sure such folks could ne'er beget
    So sweet a girl as Sally!
She is the darling of my heart,
    And she lives in our alley.

When she is by, I leave my work,
    I love her so sincerely;
My master comes like any Turk,
    And bangs me most severely;
But let him bang his bellyful,
    I'll bear it all for Sally;
She is the darling of my heart,
    And she lives in our alley.

Of all the days that's in the week
    I dearly love but one day—
And that's the day that comes betwixt
    A Saturday and Monday;
For then I'm dressed all in my best
    To walk abroad with Sally;
She is the darling of my heart,
    And she lives in our alley.

My master carries me to church,
    And often am I blamèd
Because I leave him in the lurch
    As soon as text is namèd;
I leave the church in sermon-time
    And slink away to Sally;
She is the darling of my heart,
    And she lives in our alley.

When Christmas comes about again,
    O, then I shall have money;
I'll hoard it up, and box it all,

I'll give it to my honey:
I would it were ten thousand pound,
    I'd give it all to Sally;
She is the darling of my heart,
    And she lives in our alley.

My master and the neighbours all
    Make game of me and Sally,
And, but for her, I'd better be
    A slave and row a galley;
But when my seven long years are out,
    O, then I'll marry Sally;
Oh, then we'll wed, and then we'll bed—
    But not in our alley!

Elegy Written in a Country Churchyard

Thomas Gray

Thomas Gray was born in London in 1716. He was educated at Eton and Peterhouse and apart from some European travel lived at Cambridge for the rest of his life. His father was a scrivener of unstable temperament and it was the milliner's shop kept by his mother and aunt that supplied the money for his education. His own nature was sunny as his letters show and he had a poetic gift that was at the same time popular and true. His poem, "On a Distant Prospect of Eton College" contains the famous line about the bliss of ignorance and the folly of wisdom and his famous Elegy is as full of quotations as *Hamlet*. It was so popular when it was published that he was offered the Poet Laureateship which he rejected. Instead he served from 1768 till his death as Professor of Modern History. He died in 1771 and was buried in Stoke Poges churchyard where his unoriginal but beautifully expressed elegiac thoughts had first come to him.

The curfew tolls the knell of parting day,
    The lowing herd wind slowly o'er the lea,
The plowman homeward plods his weary way,
    And leaves the world to darkness and to me.

Now fades the glimmering landscape on the sight,
    And all the air a solemn stillness holds,
Save where the beetle wheels his droning flight,
    And drowsy tinklings lull the distant folds;

Save that from yonder ivy-mantled tower
    The moping owl does to the moon complain
Of such as, wand'ring near her secret bower,
    Molest her ancient solitary reign.

Beneath those rugged elms, that yew-tree's shade,
    Where heaves the turf in many a mould'ring heap,
Each in his narrow cell for ever laid,
    The rude forefathers of the hamlet sleep.

The breezy call of incense-breathing morn,
    The swallow twitt'ring from the straw-built shed
The cock's shrill clarion, or the echoing horn,
    No more shall rouse them from their lowly bed.

For them no more the blazing hearth shall burn,
    Or busy housewife play her evening care:
No children run to lisp their sire's return,
    Or climb his knees the envied kiss to share.

Oft did the harvest to their sickle yield,
    Their furrow oft the stubborn glebe has broke:
How jocund did they drive their team afield!
    How bowed the woods beneath their sturdy stroke!

Let not Ambition mock their useful toil,
    Their homely joys, and destiny obscure;
Nor Grandeur hear with a disdainful smile
    The short and simple annals of the poor.

The boast of heraldry, the pomp of power
    And all that beauty, all that wealth e'er gave,
Awaits alike th' inevitable hour:
    The paths of glory lead but to the grave.

Nor you, ye proud, impute to These the fault,
    If Memory o'er their tomb no trophies raise,
Where through the long-drawn aisle and fretted vault
    The pealing anthem swells the note of praise.

Can storied urn or animated bust
    Back to its mansion call the fleeting breath?
Can Honour's voice provoke the silent dust,
    Or Flatt'ry soothe the dull cold ear to death?

Perhaps in this neglected spot is laid
    Some heart once pregnant with celestial fire;
Hands, that the rod of empire might have swayed,
    Or waked to ecstasy the living lyre.

But Knowledge to their eyes her ample page
    Rich with the spoils of time did ne'er unroll;
Chill Penury repressed their noble rage,
    And froze the genial current of the soul.

Full many a gem of purest ray serene
    The dark unfathomed caves of ocean bear:
Full many a flower is born to blush unseen,
    And waste its sweetness on the desert air.

Some village Hampden that with dauntless breast
    The little tyrant of his fields withstood,
Some mute inglorious Milton here may rest,
    Some Cromwell guiltless of his country's blood.

Th' applause of list'ning senates to command,
    The threats of pain and ruin to despise,
To scatter plenty o'er a smiling land,
    And read their history in a nation's eyes,

Their lot forbade: nor circumscribed alone
    Their growing virtues, but their crimes confined;
Forbade to wade through slaughter to a throne.
    And shut the gates of mercy on mankind,

The struggling pangs of conscious truth to hide,
    To quench the blushes of ingenuous shame,
Or heap the shrine of Luxury and Pride
    With incense kindled at the Muse's flame.

Far from the madding crowd's ignoble strife
    Their sober wishes never learned to stray;
Along the cool sequestered vale of life
    They kept the noiseless tenor of their way.

Yet ev'n these bones from insult to protect
    Some frail memorial still erected nigh,
With uncouth rhymes and shapeless sculpture decked,
    Implores the passing tribute of a sigh.

Their name, their years, spelt by th' unlettered Muse,
    The place of fame and elegy supply:
And many a holy text around she strews,
    That teach the rustic moralist to die.

For who, to dumb Forgetfulness a prey,
    This pleasing anxious being e'er resigned,
Left the warm precincts of the cheerful day,
    Nor cast one longing ling'ring look behind?

On some fond breast the parting soul relies,
    Some pious drops the closing eye requires;
E'en from the tomb the voice of Nature cries,
    E'en in our Ashes live their wonted fires.

For thee, who, mindful of th' unhonoured dead,
    Dost in these lines their artless tale relate;
If chance, by lonely contemplation led,
    Some kindred spirit shall inquire they fate,

Haply some hoary-headed Swain may say,
    'Oft have we seen him at the peep of dawn
Brushing with hasty steps the dews away
    To meet the sun upon the upland lawn.

'There at the foot of yonder nodding beech
    That wreathes its old fantastic roots so high,
His listless length at noontide would he stretch,
    And pore upon the brook that babbles by.

'Hard by yon wood, now smiling as in scorn,
　　Mutt'ring his wayward fancies he would rove,
Now drooping, woeful wan, like one forlorn,
　　Or crazed with care, or crossed in hopeless love.

'One morn I missed him on the customed hill,
　　Along the heath and near his fav'rite tree;
Another came; nor yet beside the rill,
Nor up the lawn, nor at the wood was he;

'The next with dirges due in sad array
Slow through the church-way path we saw him borne.
　　Approach and read (for thou canst read) the lay
Graved on the stone beneath yon aged thorn:

The Epitaph

Here rests his head upon the lap of Earth
　　A Youth to Fortune and to Fame unknown.
Fair Science frowned not on his humble birth,
　　And Melancholy marked him for her own.

Large was his bounty, and his soul sincere,
　　Heaven did a recompense as largely send:
He gave to Mis'ry all he had, a tear,
　　He gained from Heaven ('twas all he wished) a friend.

No further seek his merits to disclose,
　　Or draw his frailties from their dread abode,
(There they alike in trembling hope repose,)
　　The bosom of his Father and his God.

from The Deserted Village

Oliver Goldsmith

Oliver Goldsmith was born in Lissoy, Co Westmeath, the son of the local curate, in 1728. He graduated from Trinity after some interruptions, appearing later at the universities of Edinburgh and Leyden, and finally in London in 1756 claiming a medical qualification from Padua. In 1761 he joined the Johnson circle and survived till his death as a literary hack. He was, however, the author of classics of English literature in fiction, poetry and drama, surely a record, even for Irish versatility; and in spite of a life beset by poverty and unsuccessful gambling was notably generous. He died of the fever in 1774, mourned by his friends, Burke, Reynolds, Garrick and Dr Johnson. His poetic masterpiece, "The Deserted Village" (1770), owes much to Longford and Westmeath as do the adventures of *She Stoops to Conquer* (1773). The portrait of the parson is derived from his father, Charles, as is the main character of *The Vicar of Wakefield* (1764).

The Village Parson

Near yonder copse, where once the garden smiled,
And still where many a garden flower grows wild;
There, where a few torn shrubs the place disclose,
The village preacher's modest mansion rose.
A man he was to all the country dear,
And passing rich with forty pounds a year;
Remote from towns he ran his godly race,
Nor e'er had changed, nor wished to change his place;

Unpracticed he to fawn, or seek for power,
By doctrines fashioned to the varying hour;
Far other aims his heart had learned to prize,
More skilled to raise the wretched than to rise.
His house was known to all the vagrant train;
He chid their wanderings but relieved their pain:
The long-remembered beggar was his guest,
Whose beard descending swept his aged breast;
The ruined spendthrift, now no longer proud,
Claimed kindred there, and had his claims allowed;
The broken soldier, kindly bade to stay,
Sat by the fire, and talked the night away,
Wept o'er his wounds or, tales of sorrow done,
Shouldered his crutch and showed how fields were won.
Pleased with his guests, the good man learned to glow,
And quite forgot their vices in their woe;
Careless their merits or their faults to scan
His pity gave ere charity began.

The Village Schoolmaster

Beside yon straggling fence that skirts the way,
With blossomed furze unprofitably gay,
There, in his noisy mansion, skilled to rule,
The village master taught his little school.
A man severe he was and stern to view;
I knew him well, and every truant knew;
Well had the boding tremblers learned to trace
The day's disasters in his morning face;
Full well they laughed with counterfeited glee
At all his jokes, for many a joke had he;
Full well the busy whisper circling round
Conveyed the dismal tidings when he frowned.
Yet he was kind, or, if severe in aught,
The love he bore to learning was in fault;
The village all declared how much he knew:
'Twas certain he could write, and cipher too;
Lands he could measure, terms and tides presage,

And even the story ran that he could gauge;
In arguing, too, the parson owned his skill,
For, even though vanquished, he could argue still;
While words of learned length and thundering sound
Amazed the gazing rustics ranged around;
And still they gazed, and still the wonder grew,
That one small head could carry all he knew.

The Solitude of Alexander Selkirk

William Cowper

William Cowper was born in Berkempstead, Hertfordshire, in 1731 and bore a long life of recurring madness with great patience. He was lucky to have as patrons Morley and Mary Unwin at whose houses in Huntington and Buckingham he lived in comfort and reasonable content. Though in love with Mary and free to marry her on her husband's death he did not proceed on account of his madness. He died in 1800 having written some memorable and popular verse.

Alexander Selkirk, the subject of this famous poem, was put ashore at his own request on the uninhabited Pacific island of Juan Fernandez after a quarrel with his captain, William Dampier the privateer and not rescued until 1709 five years later. His account of his solitary stay gave Defoe the idea for his novel, *Robinson Crusoe* (1719).

> I am monarch of all I survey;
> My right there is none to dispute;
> From the centre all round to the sea
> I am lord of the fowl and the brute.
> O Solitude! where are the charms
> That sages have seen in thy face?
> Better dwell in the midst of alarms
> Then reign in this horrible place.
>
> I am out of humanity's reach,
> I must finish my journey alone,
> Never hear the sweet music of speech;
> I start at the sound of my own.

The beasts that roam over the plain
My form with indifference see;
They are so unacquainted with man,
Their tameness is shocking to me.

Society, Friendship, and Love
Divinely bestow'd upon man,
O had I the wings of a dove
How soon would I taste you again!
My sorrows I then might assuage
In the ways of religion and truth,
Might learn from the wisdom of age,
And be cheer'd by the sallies of youth.

Ye winds that have made me your sport,
Convey to this desolate shore
Some cordial endearing report
Of a land I shall visit no more:
My friends, do they now and then send
A wish or a thought after me?
O tell me I yet have a friend,
Though a friend I am never to see.

How fleet is a glance of the mind!
Compared with the speed of its flight,
The tempest itself lags behind,
And the swift-wingèd arrows of light.
When I think of my own native land
In a moment I seem to be there;
But alas! recollection at hand
Soon hurries me back to despair.

But the seafowl is gone to her nest,
The beast is laid down in his lair;
Even here is a season of rest,
And I to my cabin repair.
There's mercy in every place,
And mercy, encouraging thought!
Gives even affliction a grace
And reconciles man to his lot.

Jerusalem
from *Milton*

William Blake

William Blake was born in London in 1757 and became an engraver. When his visions drove him to write his mystic, often obscure, poetry he engraved both it and accompanying illustrations on copperplate. This poem, famous as the anthem of the Women's Institute, received new acclaim with the prizewinning film, *Chariots of Fire*. The interpretation of the poem still remains difficult and his Jerusalem is not quite as religious as it might seem. He died in 1837.

> And did those feet in ancient time
> Walk upon England's mountains green?
> And was the holy Lamb of God
> On England's pleasant pastures seen?
>
> And did the Countenance Divine
> Shine forth upon our clouded hills?
> And was Jerusalem builded here
> Among these dark Satanic Mills?
>
> Bring me my Bow of burning gold:
> Bring me my Arrows of desire:
> Bring me my Spear: O clouds unfold!
> Bring me my Chariot of fire.
>
> I will not cease from Mental Fight,
> Nor shall my Sword sleep in my hand
> Till we have built Jerusalem
> In England's green & pleasant Land.

O, My Luve is like a Red, Red Rose

Robert Burns

Robert Burns, the national bard of Scotland, was born in Alloway, Ayrshire in 1759. He was for his time and place excellently educated and far from the "illiterate plowboy genius" that he was dubbed by his Edinburgh patrons and in which he occasionally acquiesced more for devilment than for favour. He was in fact a good plowman but his other farming ventures came to nothing. His amorousness and bibulousness were not abnormal for the period and though he ran the gauntlet of Presbyterian disapproval he was and remains very popular for his humour, his egalitarianism and his perfect if not always printable love songs. "O, My Luve is like a Red, Red Rose" has become famous as a concert piece but, as the reader can easily discover, "My Bony Mary" has its own music. Its second line gave Sean O'Casey the title for his most controversial play. Burns became an exciseman in 1788 and died eight years later of rheumatic fever caught on the long, wet journeys that his duties required.

> My luve is like a red, red rose
> > That's newly sprung in June:
> My Luve is like the melodie
> > That's sweetly play'd in tune!
>
> As fair art thou, my bonnie lass,
> > So deep in Luve am I:
> And I will Luve thee still, my dear,
> > Till a' the seas gang dry:

Till a' the seas gang dry, my dear,
    And the rocks melt wi' the sun;
And I will love thee still, my dear,
    While the sands o' life shall run.

And fare-thee-weel, my only luve!
    And fare-thee-weel, a while!
And I will come again, my luve,
    Tho' it were ten thousand mile!

My Bony Mary

Robert Burns

Go, fetch to me a pint o' wine,
    And fill it in a silver tassie;
That I may drink before I go
    A service to my bonie lassie.
The boat rocks at the Pier o' Leith,
    Fu' loud the wind blaws frae the Ferry,
The ships rides by the Berwick-law,
    And I maun leave my bony Mary.

The trumpets sound, the banners fly,
    The glittering spears are ranked ready,
The shouts o' war are heard afar,
    The battle closes deep and bloody:
It's not the roar o' sea or shore,
    Wad mak me langer wish to tarry;
Nor shouts o' war that's heard afar,
    It's leaving thee, my bony Mary!

from Tintern Abbey

William Wordsworth

Wordsworth was born in Cockermouth, Cumberland in 1770, the son of a lawyer who died when William was thirteen. He was educated at St John's College, Cambridge and was in France when the Bastille was stormed. ("Bliss was it ... ") His young mistress, Annette Vallon, a daughter of a Blois surgeon, bore his child, Caroline, whom he acknowledged at the christening. He did not marry her and the headiness of revolutionary fervour was dispelled by the Terror. A sense of guilt about all aspects of the French adventure haunted him intermittently for the rest of his life. He lived in Dorset, then Somerset, and finally settled in Grasmere where, attended by his influential sister, Dorothy, he found his mature poetic voice. In 1798 he and Coleridge, with some help from Southey published the *Lyrical Ballads* and formally ushered into English poetry the Romantic Movement which had been knocking at the gate for quite sometime. He married his cousin, Mary Hutchinson, in 1802 and lived comfortably on sinecures and state pensions for the rest of his life. Dorothy never fully recovered from a breakdown in 1829 but survived her brother by five years. He became Poet Laureate in 1843 on the death of Southey and died in 1850.

The poem was written on a return visit to Tintern Abbey (a Cistercian ruin on the river Wye about five miles from Chepstow in Monmouth) on July 13, 1798. Wordsworth and Dorothy had been on "a ramble of four or five days." He wrote in his diary, "Not a line altered, nor any part of it written till I reached Bristol."

And now, with gleams of half-extinguished thought,
With many recognitions dim and faint,
And somewhat of a sad perplexity,
The picture of the mind revives again:
While here I stand, not only with the sense
Of present pleasure, but with pleasing thoughts
That in this moment there is life and food
For future years. And so I dare to hope,
Though changed no doubt, from what I was when first
I came among these hills; when like a roe
I bounded o'er the mountains, by the sides
Of the deep rivers, and the lonely streams,
Wherever nature led: more like a man
Flying from something that he dreads than one
Who sought the thing he loved. For nature then
(The coarser pleasures of my boyish days,
And their glad animal movements all gone by)
To me was all in all—I cannot paint
What then I was. The sounding cataract
Haunted me like a passion: the tall rock,
The mountain, and the deep and gloomy wood,
Their colours and their forms, were then to me
An appetite, a feeling and a love
That had no need of a remoter charm,
By thought supplied, nor any interest
Unborrowed from the eye.—That time is past,
And all its aching joys are now no more,
And all its dizzy raptures. Not for this
Faint I, nor mourn nor murmur; other gifts
have followed; for such loss, I would believe,
Abundant recompense. For I have learned
To look on nature, not as in the hour
Of thoughtless youth; but hearing oftentimes
The still, sad music of humanity,
Nor harsh nor grating, though of ample power
To chasten and subdue. And I have felt
A presence that disturbs me with the joy
Of elevated thoughts; a sense sublime
Of something far more deeply interfused,

Whose dwelling is the light of setting suns,
And the round ocean and the living air,
And the blue sky, and in the mind of man:
A motion and a spirit, that impels
All thinking things, all objects of all thought,
And rolls through all things. Therefore am I still
A lover of the meadows and the woods,
And mountains; and of all that we behold
From this green earth; of all the mighty world
Of eye, and ear,—both what they half create,
And what perceive; well pleased to recognise
In nature and the language of the sense
The anchor of my purest thoughts, the nurse,
The guide, the guardian of my heart, and soul
Of all my moral being.

Composed Upon Westminster Bridge, Sept. 3, 1802

William Wordsworth

"Composed Upon Westminster Bridge" was in fact written a month after the original experience. Dorothy's journal records: "After various troubles and disasters, we left London on Saturday morning at half past five or six, the 31st of July ... We mounted the Dover Coach at Charing Cross. It was a beautiful morning. The city, St Paul's, with the river and a multitude of little boats, made a most beautiful sight as we crossed Westminster Bridge. The houses were not overhung by their cloud of smoke, and they were spread out endlessly, yet the sun shone so brightly, with such a fierce light that there was even something like the purity of one of nature's own grand spectacles."

> Earth has not anything to show more fair:
> Dull would he be of soul who could pass by
> A sight so touching in its majesty:
> This City now doth, like a garment, wear
> The beauty of the morning; silent, bare,
> Ships, towers, domes, theatres, and temples lie
> Open unto the fields, and to the sky;
> All bright and glittering in the smokeless air.
> Never did sun more beautifully steep
> In his first splendour, valley, rock, or hill;
> Ne'er saw I, never felt, a calm so deep!
> The river glideth at his own sweet will:
> Dear God! the very houses seem asleep;
> And all that mighty heart is lying still!

The Daffodils

William Wordsworth

"The Daffodils" was written as a result of a walk on April 15, 1799, by the edge of Ullswater. Wordsworth assigns lines 21 and 22 to Mary, his wife, and says loyally but incorrectly that they are the best. It was Dorothy who pointed the sight out to the poet: "a long belt of them along the shore, about the breadth of a country turnpike road."

I wander'd lonely as a cloud
That floats on high o'er vale and hills,
When all at once I saw a crowd,
A host, of golden daffodils;
Beside the lake, beneath the trees,
Fluttering and dancing in the breeze.

Continuous as the stars that shine
And twinkle on the Milky Way,
They stretch'd in never-ending line
Along the margin of a bay:
Ten thousand saw I at a glance
Tossing their heads in sprightly dance.

The waves beside them danced, but they
Out-did the sparkling waves in glee:
A poet could not but be gay
In such a jocund company:
I gazed—and gazed—but little thought
What wealth the show to me had brought:

For oft, when on my couch I lie
In vacant or in pensive mood,
They flash upon that inward eye
Which is the bliss of solitude;
And then my heart with pleasure fills,
And dances with the daffodils.

Lochinvar

Sir Walter Scott

Sir Walter Scott was born in Edinburgh in 1771 and graduated from the university there as an advocate. His frequent professional travels in the Border country led to an unsurpassed collection of ballads, *Minstrelsy for the Scottish Border* (1803) and his own poetry was a tribute to the romance and strength of these survivals. His Waverley novels gained him international fame but he killed himself with overwork paying off his company's debts. He died in 1832.

"Lochinvar" is a typical literary ballad, too polished and lacking the vigour and crudity of the older models. It is still his best known poem though nowadays the use of the sobriquet "Young Lochinvar" is invariably comic.

> O, young Lochinvar is come out of the west,
> Through all the wide Border his steed was the best;
> And save his good broadsword he weapons had none,
> He rode all unarmed, and he rode all alone.
> So faithful in love, and so dauntless in war,
> There never was knight like the young Lochinvar.
>
> He staid not for brake, and he stopped not for stone.
> He swam the Eske river where ford there was none;
> But ere he alighted at Netherby gate,
> The bride had consented, the gallant came late:
> For a laggard in love, and a dastard in war,
> Was to wed the fair Ellen of brave Lochinvar.
>
> So boldly he entered the Netherby Hall,
> Among bride's-men, and kinsmen, and brothers, and all:

Then spoke the bride's father, his hand on his sword,
(For the poor craven bridegroom said never a word,)
'O come ye in peace here, or come ye in war,
Or to dance at our bridal, young Lord Lochinvar?

"I long wooed your daughter my suit you denied;—
Love swells like the Solway, but ebbs like its tide—
And now am I come, with this lost love of mine,
To lead but one measure, drink one cup of wine.
There are maidens in Scotland more lovely by far,
That would gladly be bride to the young Lochinvar."

The bride kissed the goblet: the knight took it up,
He quaffed off the wine, and he threw down the cup.
She looked down to blush, and she looked up to sigh,
With a smile on her lips, and a tear in her eye.
He took her soft hand, ere her mother could bar,—
"Now tread we a measure!" said young Lochinvar.

So stately his form, and so lovely her face,
That never a hall such a galliard did grace;
While her mother did fret, and her father did fume.
And the bridgegroom stood dangling his bonnet and plume;
And the bride-maidens whispered "'Twere better by far,
To have matched our fair cousin with your Lochinvar."

One touch to her hand, and one word in her ear,
When they reached the hall-door, and the charger stood near;
So light to the croupe the fair lady he swung,
So light to the saddle before her he sprung!
"She is won! we are gone, over bank, bush, and scare;
They'll have fleet steeds that follow," quoth young Lochinvar.

There was mounting 'mong Graemes of the Netherby clan;
Forsters, Fenwicks, and Musgraves, they rode and they ran:
There was racing and chasing on Cannobie Lee,
But the lost bride of Netherby ne'er did they see.
So daring in love, and so dauntless in war,
Have ye e'er hear of gallant like young Lochinvar?—

Kubla Khan

Samuel Taylor Coleridge

Samuel Taylor Coleridge was born in 1772 at Ottery St Mary in Devonshire where his father was vicar, and educated at Christ's Hospital, London, where he first met his friend, Charles Lamb. He was by turn editor, Unitarian minister, translator, critic and poet. He suffered continually from toothache and neuralgia which led to opium addiction, a common crutch at the time. He was one of the founders of the Romantic Movement in England and still remains a fine interpreter of Shakespeare. He spent the last twenty-five years of his life in the home of various friends, including the Wedgewoods and the Wordsworths. He died in his sleep in the summer of 1834 at the home of a friend, James Gilman, a surgeon of Highgate. He was, in the description of his dear friend, Lamb, "an archangel, a little damaged."

"Kubla Khan" is famous for not being finished. Coleridge was reading an account of the travels of Marco Polo and of his meeting with the Khan Kubla of Tartary when he fell into one of his heavy opiate sleeps. On waking he wrote these few hundred lines but was interrupted by an unnamed "person from Porlock" (a neighbouring village across the Devon border) and could not remember the rest. The Porlock Person has become a metaphor for the many who distract an artist from his work. The critic J Livingstone Lowes has traced all the images used by Coleridge in his famous book. *The Road to Xanadu*(1927)

In Xanadu did Kubla Khan
A stately pleasure-dome decree:
Where Alph, the sacred river, ran
Through caverns measureless to man
    Down to a sunless sea.
So twice five miles of fertile ground
With walls and towers were girdled round:
And here were gardens bright with sinuous rills,
Where blossomed many an incense-bearing tree;
And here were forests ancient as the hills,
Enfolding sunny spots of greenery.

But oh! that deep romantic chasm which slanted
Down the green hill athwart a cedarn cover!
A savage place! as holy and enchanted
As e'er beneath a waning moon was haunted
By woman wailing for her demon-lover!
And from this chasm, with ceaseless turmoil seething
As if this earth in fast thick pants were breathing,
A mighty fountain momently was forced:
Amid whose swift half-intermitted burst
Huge fragments vaulted like rebounding hail
Or chaffy grain beneath the thresher's flail:
And mid these dancing rocks at once and ever
It flung up momently the sacred river,
Five miles meandering with a mazy motion
Through wood and dale the sacred river ran.
Then reached the caverns measureless man,
And sank in tumult to a lifeless ocean:
And 'mid this tumult Kubla heard from far
Ancestral voices prophesying war!

    The shadow of the dome of pleasure
    Floated midway on the waves;
    Where was heard the mingled measure
    From the fountain and the caves
It was a miracle of rare device,
A sunny pleasure-dome with caves of ice!

A damsel with a dulcimer
  In vision once I saw:
      It was an Abyssinian maid,
      And on her dulcimer she played,
      Singing of Mount Abora.
      Could I revive within me
      Her symphony and song,
      To such a deep delight 'twould win me,
That with music loud and long,
I would build that dome in air,
That sunny dome! those caves of ice!
And all who heard should see them there,
And all should cry, Beware! Beware!
His flashing eyes, his floating hair!
Weave a circle round him thrice,
And close your eyes with holy dread,
For he on honey-dew hath fed,
And drunk the milk of Paradise.

The Old Familiar Faces

Charles Lamb (1775-1834)

Charles Lamb was born in 1775 in London and educated at Christ's hospital where he met Coleridge, a lifelong friend. He became a clerk in the East India house in 1792 and remained there till 1825 when he became the "superannuated man" of his famous essay. The central fact of his life was the tragic killing of their mother by his sister Mary in a fit of madness in 1796. She was released into his care but their circumstances were such that marriage was precluded for him. Lamb became the most famous essayist in English literature writing under the psueudonym "Elia," the name of an Italian fellow clerk, "a gay, light-hearted foreigner." In spite of his cross (Mary's madness was recurring) Lamb managed to remain tolerably light-hearted himself and was loved by his many friends. He died of erysipelas in 1834 in the village of Edmonton in Middlesex.

Though famous as an essayist and regarded as the finest critic of Elizabethan and Jacobean literature of his day, Lamb wrote some very appealing poems of which this is the best known. It was, however, written in 1798 when Lamb was only twenty-three. This bears out a remark of one of his friends that Elia was a nice old fellow who would never age because he was never young.

> I have had playmates, I have had companions,
> In my days of childhood, in my joyful school-days—
> All, all are gone, the old familiar faces.

I have been laughing, I have been carousing,
Drinking late, sitting late, with my bosom cronies—
All, all are gone, the old familiar faces.

I loved a love once, fairest among women.
Closed are her doors on me, I must not see her—
All, all are gone, the old familiar faces.

I have a friend, a kinder friend has no man.
Like an ingrate, I left my friend abruptly;
Left him, to muse on the old familiar faces.

Ghost-like, I paced round the haunts of my childhood.
Earth seem'd a desert I was bound to traverse,
Seeking to find the old familiar faces.

Friend of my bosom, thou more that brother!
Why were not thou born in my father's dwelling?
So might we talk of the old familiar faces.

How some they have died, and some they have left me,
And some are taken from me; all are departed;
All, all are gone, the old familiar faces.

I Saw from the Beach

Thomas Moore

Thomas Moore was born in Dublin in 1779, educated at Trinity College where he was friendly with Emmet and other United Irishmen and, though he took no part in the '98 Rising, remained a firm if constitutional nationalist all his life. He was a gifted light poet and more highly regarded in his time than his close friend, Byron. His lasting legacy are the *Irish Melodies* which are a miraculously graceful marriage of words to melody. He died after a period of premature senility in Wiltshire in 1852. He was one of Ireland's finest ambassadors at a time when such was greatly needed.

"The Minstrel Boy" and "She is Far from the Land" are patent tributes to Robert Emmet and his romantic love, Sarah Curran. "I Saw from the Beach" may not strike one as very moving as the words lie somewhat inert on the printed page, but sung with the right tenor voice to the tune, "Miss Molly," they can wring the tears as few others can.

I saw from the beach, when the morning was shining,
    A bark o'er the waters move gloriously on;
I came when the sun from that beach was declining,
    The bark was still there, but the waters were gone.

And such is the fate of our life's early promise,
    So passing the spring-tide of joy we have known;
Each wave, that we danc'd on at morning, ebbs from us,
    And leaves us, at eve, on the bleak shore alone.

Ne'er tell me of glories, serenely adorning
    The close of our day, the calm eve of our night;—
Give me back, give me back the wild freshness of Morning,
    Her clouds and her tears are wild Evening's best light.

The Minstrel Boy

Thomas Moore

The Minstrel Boy to the war is gone,
   In the ranks of death you'll find him;
His father's sword he had girded on,
   And his wild harp slung behind him—
"Land of song!" said the warrior-bard,
   "Though all the world betrays thee,
One sword, at least, thy rights shall guard,
   One faithful harp shall praise thee!"

The Minstrel fell!—but the foeman's chain
   Could not bring his proud soul under;
The harp he loved ne'er spoke again,
   For he tore its chords asunder;
And said, "No chains shall sully thee,
   Thou soul of love and bravery!
They songs were made for the pure and free,
   They shall never sound in slavery."

She is Far from the Land

Thomas Moore

She is far from the land where her young hero sleeps,
    And lovers are round her, sighing:
But coldly she turns from their gaze, and weeps,
    For her heart in his grave is lying.

She sings the wild song of her dear native plains,
    Every note which he loved awaking;—
Ah! little they think who delight in her strains,
    How the heart of the Minstrel is breaking.

He had lived for his love, for his country he died,
    They were all that to life had entwined him;
Nor soon shall the tears of his country be dried,
    Nor long will his love stay behind him.

Oh! make her a grave where the sunbeams rest,
    When they promise a glorious morrow;
They'll shine o'er her sleep, like a smile from the West,
    From her own loved island of sorrow.

Abou Ben Adhem

James Henry Leigh Hunt

Leigh Hunt was born in 1784 in Southgate, Middlesex, and after schooling at Christ's Hospital became a radical journalist. He was a friend of Byron, the first publisher of Shelley and Keats and a charming essayist. His wife was something of a domestic disaster and his children ran wild, usually in other people's houses, He was a gentle, superficial man whose aesthetic heart was in the right place. He died in 1859 having outlived most of his more gifted friends "Abou Ben Adhem" a story from Rabbinical lore, was published quite appropriately in *The Book of Gems* in 1838.

Abou Ben Adhem (may his tribe increase!)
Awoke one night from a deep dream of peace,
And saw, within the moonlight in his room,
Making it rich, and like a lily in bloom,
An angel writing in a book of gold:—
Exceeding peace had made Ben Adhem bold,
And to the presence in the room he said,
  "What writest thou?"—The vision raised its head,
And with a look made of all sweet accord,
Answered, "The names of those that love the Lord."
  "And is mine one?" said Abou. "Nay, not so,"
Replied the angel. Abou spoke more low,
But cheerly still; and said, "I pray thee, then,
Write me as one that loves his fellow men."
  The angel wrote, and vanished. The next night
It came again with a great wakening light,
And showed the names whom love of God had blessed,
And lo! Ben Adhem's name led all the rest.

So, We'll Go No More A-Roving

Lord Byron

George Gordon, Lord Byron, was born in 1778. He went to Harrow and Trinity College, Cambridge, where in spite of a club foot he excelled at sport. His poem *Childe Harold's Pilgrimage*, completed in 1818, made him famous, but already he had been characterised by one of his mistresses as "mad, bad and dangerous to know." His narrative poetry created the Byronic hero, of which he, with his travels, dissipation and good looks, was a type. He stood for all the more theatrical aspects of the Romantic Revival but his poetry is rather Augustan than like the other Romantics. He restored his reputation by his courageous involvement in the Greek War of Independence against the Turks and died of rheumatic fever at Missolonghi in 1824. His body was carried by warship home to a hero's funeral in England.
"So, We'll Go No More A-Roving" strikes a chord in the heart of every retired rake, and of many who never attained to that status.

> So, we'll go no more a-roving
>   So late into the night,
> Though the heart be still as loving,
>   And the moon be still as bright.
>
> For the sword outwears its sheath,
>   And the soul wears out the breast,
> And the heart must pause to breathe,
>   And love itself have rest.
>
> Though the night was made for loving,
>   And the day returns too soon,
> Yet we'll go no more a-roving
>   By the light of the moon.

The Destruction of Sennacherib

Lord Byron

The story of Sennacherib, who was King of Assyria from 705 to 681 BC is told in 2 Kings Chapter 19: "And it came to pass that night, that the angel of the Lord went out, and smote in the camp of the Assyrians an hundred fourscore and five thousand: And when they arose early in the morning, behold they were all dead corpses."

The Assyrian came down like the wolf on the fold,
And his cohorts were gleaming in purple and gold;
And the sheen of their spears was like stars on the sea,
When the blue wave rolls nightly on deep Galilee.

Like the leaves of the forest when Summer is green,
That host with the banners at sunset were seen:
Like the leaves of the forest when Autumn hath blow,
That host on the morrow lay withered and strown.

For the Angel of Death spread his wings on the blast,
And breathed in the face of the foe as he passed;
And the eyes of the sleepers waxed deadly and chill,
And their hearts but once heaved, and for ever grew still.

And there lay the steed with his nostril all wide,
But through it there rolled not the breath of his pride:
And the foam of his gasping lay white on the turf,
And cold as the spray of the rock-beating surf.

And there lay the rider distorted and pale,
With the dew on his brow and the rust on his mail;
And the tents were all silent, the banners alone,
The lances unlifted, the trumpet unblown.

And the widows of Ashur are loud in their wail,
And the idols are broke in the temple of Baal;
And the might of the Gentile, unsmote by the sword,
Hath melted like snow in the glance of the Lord!

Ozymandias

P.B. Shelley

Percy Bysshe Shelley was born in Sussex in 1792 and educated at Eton and University College, Oxford. In 1811 he married the sixteen-year-old Harriet Westbrook. They lived in poverty for a while until both fathers relented and made them an allowance of £400 each. In 1814 he eloped with Mary Godwin and married her in 1816 after Harriet had drowned herself in the Serpentine. The Shelleys moved to Italy and gathered a coterie of poets about them, notably Byron and Keats. In 1821 they settled in Lerici and it was there that he was drowned in a sailing accident. He was buried in Rome near his friend Keats.

"Ozymandias" was written in 1818, the broken statue being that of Rameses II whose tomb at Thebes in Upper Egypt was as famous a wonder as the Pyramids.

> I met a traveller from an antique land
> Who said: Two vast and trunkless legs of stone
> Stand in the desert. Near them, on the sand,
> Half sunk, a shatter'd visage lies, whose frown,
> And wrinkled lip, and sneer of cold command,
> Tell that its sculptor well those passions read
> Which yet survive, stamp'd on these lifeless things,
> The hand that mock'd them and heart that fed:
> And on the pedestal these words appear:
> "My name is Ozymandias, king of kings:
> Look on my works, ye Mighty, and despair!"
> Nothing beside remains, Round the decay
> Of that colossal wreck, boundless and bare
> The lone and level sands stretch far away.

Ode to the West Wind

P.B. Shelley.

This marvellous poem was written in Florence in the woods along the Arno in 1819. It consists of five sonnets and displays supreme poetic technique in rhyme and assonance and a wonderful sense of the triumph of hope over despair.

O wild West Wind, thou breath of Autumn's being,
Thou, from whose unseen presence the leaves dead
Are driven, like ghosts from an enchanter fleeing,
Yellow, and black, and pale, and hectic red,
Pestilence-stricken multitudes: O thou
Who chariotest to their dark wintry bed
The winged seed, where they lie cold and low,
Each like a corpse within its grave, until
Thine azure sister of the spring shall blow
Her clarion o'er the dreaming earth, and fill
(Driving sweet buds like flocks to feed in air)
With living hues and odours plain and hill:
Wild Spirit, which art moving everywhere;
Destoyer and Preserver; Hear, O hear!

Thou on whose stream, 'mid the steep sky's commotion,
Loose clouds like earth's decaying leaves are shed
Shook from the tangled boughs of Heaven and Ocean,
Angels of rain and lightning; there are spread
On the blue surface of thine airy surge,
Like the bright hair uplifted from the head
Of some fierce Maenad, ev'n from the dim verge

Of the horizon to the zenith's height—
The locks of the approaching storm. Thou dirge
Of the dying year, to which this closing night
Will be the dome of a vast sepulchre
Vaulted with all thy congregated might
Of vapours, from whose solid atmosphere
Black rain, and fire, and hail, will burst: O hear!

Thou who didst waken from his summer-dreams
The blue Mediterranean, where he lay
Lull'd by the coil of his crystalline streams
Beside a pumice isle in Baiae's bay,
And saw in sleep old palaces and towers
Quivering within the wave's intenser day,
All overgrown with azure moss and flowers
So sweet, the sense faints picturing them! Thou
For whose path the Atlantic's level powers
Cleave themselves into chasms, while far below
The sea-blooms and the oozy woods which wear
The sapless foliage of the ocean, know
Thy voice, and suddenly grow gray with fear
And tremble and despoil themselves: O hear!

If I were a dead leaf thou mightest bear;
If I were a swift cloud to fly with thee;
A wave to pant beneath thy power, and share
The impulse of thy strength, only less free
Than Thou, O uncontrollable! If even
I were as in my boyhood, and could be
The comrade of thy wanderings over heaven,
As then, when to outstrip the skyey speed
Scarce seem'd a vision, I would ne'er have striven
As thus with thee in prayer in my sore need.
O lift me as a wave, a leaf, a cloud!
I fall upon the thorns of life! I bleed!
A heavy weight of hours had chain'd and bow'd
One too like thee: tameless, and swift, and proud.

Make me thy lyre, ev'n as the forest is:
What if my leaves are falling like its own!
The tumult of thy mighty harmonies
Will take from both a deep autumnal tone,
Sweet though in sadness. Be thou, Spirit fierce,
My spirit! be thou me, impetuous one!
Drive my dead thoughts over the universe
Like wither'd leaves to quicken a new birth;
And, by the incantation of this verse,
Scatter, as from an unextinguish'd hearth
Ashes and sparks, my words among mankind!
Be through my lips to unawaken'd earth
The trumpet of a prophecy! O Wind,
If Winter comes, can Spring be far behind?

Abide with Me

H.F. Lyte

Henry Francis Lyte was born in Kelso in 1793, educated at Trinity College, Dublin, took orders and became vicar of Lower Brixham in Devon. He published *Poems, Chiefly Religious* in 1833 but he is now only known for this hymn which has a funeral dignity possessed by few others. He died in 1847.

Abide with me; fast falls the eventide;
The darkness deepens; Lord, with me abide.
When other helpers fail, and comforts flee,
Help of the helpless, O abide with me!

Swift to its close ebbs out life's little day;
Earth's joys grow dim, its glories pass away:
Change and decay in all around I see,
O Thou who changest not, abide with me.

Not a brief glance I beg, a passing word;
But as Thou dweltst with Thy disciples, Lord,
Familiar, condescending, patient, free,—
Come, not to sojourn, but abide with me.

Come not in terrors, as the King of kings;
But kind and good, with healing in Thy wings,
Tears for all woes, a heart for every plea,
Come, Friend of sinners, and thus bide with me.

Thou on my head in early youth didst smile
And, though rebellious and perverse meanwhile,
Thou hast not left me, oft as I left Thee,
On to the close, O Lord, abide with me!

I need Thy presence every passing hour;
What but Thy grace can foil the tempter's power?
Who like Thyself my guide and stay can be?
Through cloud and sunshine, Lord, abide with me.

I fear no foe with Thee at hand to bless;
Ills have no weight and tears no bitterness;
Where is death's sting? Where, grave, thy victory?
I triumph still if Thou abide with me.

Hold Thou Thy cross before my closing eyes;
Shine through the gloom and point me to the skies!
Heaven's morning breaks and earth's vain shadows flee;
In life, in death, O Lord, abide with me.

On First Looking into Chapman's Homer

John Keats

John Keats was born in London in 1795 and began medical studies in Guy's Hospital where he later qualified as a surgeon. His early work, including this famous sonnet was published by Leigh Hunt but when it appeared in book form it was not very well received. Later work was savaged by the *Edinburgh Review* when he was too ill to deal with the attack. He was already dying with tuberculosis when he accepted Shelley's invitation to live in Italy but he died in February 1821 at the age of twenty-five. He is the most sensuous poet after Shakespeare and though his early death makes full critical judgement impossible one might safely have claimed much for him.

Much have I travell'd in the realms of gold,
    And many goodly states and kingdoms seen;
    Round many western islands have I been
Which bards in fealty to Apollo hold.
Oft of one wide expanse had I been told
    That deep-brow'd Homer ruled as his demesne;
    Yet did I never breathe its pure serene
Till I heard Chapman speak out loud and bold:
Then felt I like some watcher of the skies
    When a new planet swims into his ken;
Or like stout Cortez when with eagle eyes
    He stared at the Pacific—and all his men
Look'd at each other with a wild surmise—
    Silent, upon a peak in Darien.

Ode to a Nightingale

John Keats

"Ode to a Nightingale" was written in 1819 in a garden in the Hampstead house that is now the Keats Museum. He sat under a tree writing it on bits of paper. It is heavy with foreboding of early death.

My heart aches, and a drowsy numbness pains
    My sense, as though of hemlock I had drunk,
Or emptied some dull opiate to the drains
    One minute past, and Lethe-wards had sunk:
'Tis not through envy of thy happy lot,
    But being too happy in thine happiness,—
        That thou, light-winged Dryad of the trees,
        In some melodious plot
Of beechen green, and shadows numberless,
    Singest of summer in full-throated ease.

O, for a draught of vintage! that hath been
    Cool'd a long age in the deep-delved earth,
Tasting of Flora and the country green
    Dance, and Provençal song, and sunburnt mirth!
O for a beaker full of the warm South,
    Full of the true, the blushful Hippocrene,
        With beaded bubbles winking at the brim,
        And purple-stained mouth;
That I might drink and leave the world unseen,
    And with thee fade away into the forest dim:

Fade far away, dissolve, and quite forget
    What thou among the leaves hast never known,
The weariness, the fever, and the fret
    Here, where men sit and hear each other groan;
Where palsy shakes a few, sad, last gray hairs,
    Where youth grows pale, and spectre-thin, and dies;
        Where but to think is to be full of sorrow
          And leaden-eyed despairs,
Where Beauty cannot keep her lustrous eyes,
    Or new Love pine at them beyond to-morrow.

Away! away! for I will fly to thee,
    Not charioted by Bacchus and his pards,
But on the viewless wings of Poesy,
    Though the dull brain perplexes and retards:
Already with thee! tender is the night,
    And haply the Queen-Moon is on her throne,
        Cluster'd around by all her starry Fays;
          But here there is no light,
Save what from heaven is with the breezes blown
    Through verdurous glooms and winding mossy ways.

I cannot see what flowers are at my feet,
    Nor what soft incense hangs upon the boughs,
But, in embalmed darkness, guess each sweet
    Wherewith the seasonable month endows
The grass, the thicket, and the fruit-tree wild;
    White hawthorn, and the pastoral eglantine;
        Fast fading violets cover'd up in leaves;
          And mid-May's eldest child,
The coming musk-rose, full of dewy wine,
    The murmurous haunt of flies on summer eves.

Darkling I listen; and, for many a time
    I have been half in love with easeful Death,
Call'd him soft names in many a mused rhyme,
    To take into the air my quiet breath;
Now more than ever seems it rich to die,
    To cease upon the midnight with no pain,

While thou art pouring forth thy soul abroad
    In such an ecstasy!
Still wouldst thou sing, and I have ears in vain—
    To thy high requiem become a sod.

Thou wast not born for death, immortal Bird!
    No hungry generations tread thee down;
The voice I hear this passing night was heard
    In ancient days by emperor and clown:
Perhaps the self-same song that found a path
    Through the sad heart of Ruth, when, sick for home,
      She stood in tears amid the alien corn;
        The same that oft-times hath
Charm'd magic casements,opening on the foam
    Of perilous seas, in faery lands forlorn.

Forlorn! the very word is like a bell
    To toll me back from thee to my sole self!
Adieu! the fancy cannot cheat so well
    As she is fam'd to do, deceiving elf.
Adieu! adieu thy plaintive anthem fades
    Past the near meadows, over the still stream,
      Up the hill-side; and now 'tis buried deep
      In the next valley-glades:
Was it a vision, or a waking dream?
    Fled is that music:—Do I wake or sleep?

I remember, I remember

Thomas Hood

Thomas Hood was born in London in 1799, the son of a Scottish bookseller. He began his adult work as an engraver and when he became a humorous writer often illustrated his work with comic drawings. He lacked the savagery to be a satirist and his friend, Charles Lamb, called him "our half-Hogarth." He was editor of many magazines but fought an increasingly losing battle with tuberculosis. His comic poems depend mainly upon his tremendous capacity for puns but it was his serious work which was most popular during his lifetime. This popular but very sentimental poem was published in his last collection, "The Plea of the Midsummer Fairies," in 1839. He died in 1845 having successfully obtained a Civil List pension for *his wife*.

> I remember, I remember,
> The house where I was born,
> The little window where the sun
> Came peeping in at morn;
> He never came a wink too soon,
> Nor brought too long a day;
> But now, I often wish the night
> Had borne my breath away!
>
> I remember, I remember,
> The roses, red and white,
> The violets, and the lily-cups—
> Those flowers made of light!
> The lilacs where the robin built,

And where my brother set
The laburnum on his birthday,—
The tree is living yet!

I remember, I remember,
Where I was used to swing,
And thought the air must rush as fresh
To swallows on the wing;
My spirit flew in feathers then
That is so heavy now,
And summer pools could hardly cool
The fever on my brow.

I remember, I remember,
The fir-trees dark and high;
I used to think their slender tops
Were close against the sky:
It was a childish ignorance,
But now 'tis little joy
To know I'm farther off from heaven
Than when I was a boy.

Concord Hymn

Ralph Waldo Emerson

Ralph Waldo Emerson was born in Boston in 1803. His essays were as popular in New England as Lamb's were in England. He died in 1882, famous among non-literary people as the coiner of the motto, "Hitch your wagon to a star."

The War of Independence, threatening for several years, actually broke out in the New Hampshire town of Concord when armed colonists faced a detachment of British soldiers on 19 April 1775. The verse was written to celebrate a memorial unveiled on Independence Day, more than sixty years later.

Sung at the completion of the Battle Monument, July 4, 1837

> By the rude bridge that arched the flood,
>   Their flags to April's breeze unfurled,
> Here once the embattled farmers stood
>   And fired the shot heard round the world.
>
> The foe long since in silence slept;
>   Alike the conqueror silent sleeps;
> And Time the ruined bridge has swept
>   Down the dark stream which seaward creeps.
>
> On this green bank, by this soft stream,
>   We set to-day a votive stone;
> That memory may their deed redeem,
>   When, like our sires, our sons are gone.
>
> Spirit, that made those heroes dare
>   To die, and leave their children free,
> Bid Time and Nature gentle spare
>   The shaft we raise to them and thee.

How Do I Love Thee?

Elizabeth Browning

Elizabeth Barrett Browning was born in Durham in 1806 but after several addresses settled into the role of semi-invalid as she lived with her father and large family in Wimpole Street, in London. She was an omnivorous reader and a published poet when the unknown Robert Browning came to visit her and literally swept her off her feet. She married him in 1846 in spite of morbid opposition from her father and they lived happily and healthily in Italy for fifteen years. She is now best remembered for her sonnets which describe her own feeling for her adored husband. She was a feminist in advance of her time though her practice, especially in her treatment of her own servants did not live up to her stated ideals. She died in Florence in 1861.

How do I love thee? Let me count the ways.
I love thee to the depth and breadth and height
My soul can reach, when feeling out of sight
For the ends of Being and ideal Grace.
I love thee to the level of every day's
Most quiet need, by sun and candlelight.
I love thee freely, as men strive for Right;
I love thee purely, as they turn from Praise.
I love thee with the passion put to use
In my old griefs, and with my childhood's faith.
I love thee with a love I seemed to lose
With my lost saints,—I love thee with the breath,
Smiles, tears, of all my life!—and, if God chooses,
I shall but love thee better after death.

The Irish Emigrant

Helena Dufferin

Helena, Lady Dufferin, was born Sheridan in London in 1807, the grand-daughter of the Dublin wit and dramatist, Richard Brinsley Sheridan. She married Commander Blackwood in 1825 and became Countess Dufferin on her husband's succession to the Co. Down seat in 1839. She inherited the Sheridan wit and way with a song. She also wrote the famous "Bay of Dublin." She died in 1867.

I'm sitting on the stile, Mary,
    Where we sat, side by side,
That bright May morning long ago
    When first you were my bride.
The corn was springing fresh and green,
    And the lark sang loud and high,
The red was on your lip, Mary,
    The love-light in your eye.

The place is little changed, Mary,
    The day is bright as then,
The lark's loud song is in my ear,
    The corn is green again;
But I miss the soft clasp of your hand,
    Your breath warm on my cheek,
And I still keep list'ning for the words
    You never more may speak.

'Tis but a step down yonder land,
   The little Church stands near—
The Church where we were wed, Mary—
   I see the spire from here;
But the graveyard lies between, Mary—
   My step might break your rest—
Where you, my darling, lie asleep
   With your baby on your breast.

I'm very lonely now, Mary—
   The poor make no new friends—
But, oh, they love the better still
   The few our Father sends.
And you were all I had, Mary,
   My blessing and my pride;
There's nothing left to care for now,
   Since my poor Mary died.

Yours was the good brave heart, Mary,
   That still kept hoping on,
When trust in God had left my soul,
   And half my strength was gone.
There was comfort ever on your lip,
   And the kind look on your brow.
I bless you, Mary, for that same,
   Though you can't hear me now.

I thank you for the patient smile
   When your heart was fit to break;
When the hunger pain was gnawing there
   You hid it for my sake!
I bless you for the pleasant word,
   When your heart was sad and sore.
Oh! I'm thankful you are gone Mary,
   Where grief can't reach you more!

The Village Blacksmith

Henry Wadsworth Longfellow

Henry Wadsworth Longfellow was born in Portland, Maine in 1807, the son of a lawyer. His father was a trustee of Bowdoin College and the son was appointed to the new chair of Modern Languages. He wisely engaged on a European tour of study which lasted three years. He was appointed to the same chair at Harvard in 1835 and for sixteen influential years was its most famous faculty member. His first wife, Mary Potter, died in Amsterdam in 1836. He remarried in 1843 by which time his work was as popular as Tennyson's. This second wife, Frances Appleton, was burned to death in 1861, a tragedy which told heavily upon him. This famous, and frequently parodied, poem, was written in 1841. Other famous accessible and also parodied works are "Paul Revere's Ride" (1863) and "The Song of Hiawatha" (1858) that even the people of Minnesota laugh at. He died in 1882.

> Under a spreading chestnut-tree
>   The village smithy stands,
> The smith, a mighty man is he,
>   With large and sinewy hands;
> And the muscles of his brawny arms
>   Are strong as iron bands.
>
> His hair is crisp, and black, and long,
>   His face is like the tan;
> His brow is wet with honest sweat,
>   He earns whate'er he can,
> And looks the whole world in the face,
>   For he owes not any man.

Week in, week out, from morn till night,
   You can hear his bellows blow;
You can hear him swing his heavy sledge,
   With measured beat and slow,
Like a sexton ringing the village bell,
   When the evening sun is low.

And children coming home from school
   Look in at the open door;
They love to see the flaming forge,
   And hear the bellows roar,
And catch the burning sparks that fly
   Like chaff from a threshing-floor.

He goes on Sunday to the church,
   And sits among his boys;
He hears the parson pray and preach,
   He hears his daughter's voice
Singing in the village choir,
   And it makes his heart rejoice;

It sounds to him like her mother's voice,
   Singing in Paradise!
He needs must think of her once more,
   How in the grave she lies;
And with his hard, rough hand he wipes
   A tear out of his eyes.

Toiling,—rejoicing,—sorrowing,
   Onward through life he goes;
Each morning sees some task begun,
   Each evening sees its close!
Something attempted, something done,
   Has earned a night's repose.

Thanks, thanks to thee, my worthy friend,
   For the lesson thou hast taught!
Thus at the flaming forge of life
   Our fortune must be wrought;
Thus on its sounding anvil shaped
   Each burning deed and thought.

Barbara Frietchie

John Greenleaf Whittier

John Greenleaf Whittier was born in Haverhill, Massachusetts in 1807, the son of Quaker small farmers. He was a strong anti-slavery activist and became widely known as an abolitionist because of such poems as "Barbara Frietchie," which was written at the height of the Civil War. After the struggle he retired to Amesbury, Mass. and wrote mainly rural and nature poetry. He died in 1892.

> Up from the meadows rich with corn,
> Clear in the cool September morn,
> The clustered spires of Frederick stand
> Green-walled by the hills of Maryland.
> Round about them orchards sweep,
> Apple and peach tree fruited deep,
> Fair as the garden of the Lord
> To the eyes of the famished rebel horde,
> On that pleasant morn of the early fall
> When Lee marched over the mountain-wall;
> Over the mountains winding down,
> Horse and foot, into Frederick town.
>
> Forty flags with their silver stars,
> Forty flags with their crimson bars,
> Flapped in the morning wind: the sun
> Of noon looked down, and saw not one.
> Up rose old Barbara Frietchie then,
> Bowed with her fourscore years and ten;
> Bravest of all in Frederick town
> She took up the flag the men hauled down;
> In her attic window the staff she set,
> To show that one heart was loyal yet.

Up the street came the rebel tread,
Stonewall Jackson riding ahead.
Under his slouched hat left and right
He glanced; the old flag met his sight.
"Halt!"—the dust-brown ranks stood fast.
"Fire!"—out blazed the rifle-blast.
It shivered the window, pane and sash;
It rent the banner with seam and gash.
Quick, as it fell, from the broken staff
Dame Barbara snatched the silken scarf.
She leaned far out on the window-sill,
And shook it forth with a royal will.
"Shoot if you must, this old gray head,
But spare your country's flag," she said.

A shade of sadness, a blush of shame,
Over the face of the leader came;
The nobler nature within him stirred
To life at that woman's deed and word;
"Who touches a hair of yon gray head
Dies like a dog! march on!" he said.
All day long through Frederick street
Sounded the tread of marching feet:
All day long that free flag tost
Over the heads of the rebel host.
Ever its torn folds rose and fell
On the loyal winds that loved it well;
And through the hill-gaps sunset light
Shone over it with a warm good-night.

Barbara Frietchie's work is o'er,
And the Rebel rides on his raids no more.
Honour to her! and let a tear
Fall, for her sake, on Stonewall's bier.
Over Barbara Frietchie's grave,
Flag of Freedom and Union, wave!
Pace and order and beauty draw
Round thy symbol of light and law;
And ever the stars above look down
On thy stars below in Frederick town!

from The Rubá'iyát of Omar Khayyám of Naishápúr

Edward Fitzgerald

Edward Fitzgerald was born in Suffolk in 1809, the third son in a family of eight. He was educated at Bury St. Edmunds Grammar School and Trinity College, Cambridge, where he was a close friend of Thackeray. He later cultivated the friendship of Tennyson. He never engaged in any profession nor strayed far from his native shire and his one marital adventure, with the daughter of the subject of his first book, Bernard Barton, lasted barely a year. He preferred to spend his time sailing with the fishermen of Lowestoft. His great claim to fame is his translation of the quatrains (*rubais*) of the Persian poet, Omar the Tentmaker. Perhaps "version" is a more accurate word than "translation" though modern scholars admit that he caught the spirit of the original well. It was a tremendously popular book with the Victorians who loved a sanitised Orient and could ignore the knotty fact that Omar's beloved was a boy. Fitzgerald died in 1893 after a life more than somewhat happy if one can gauge by his jolly letters.

> Awake! for Morning in the Bowl of Night
> Has flung the Stone that puts the Stars to flight:
>   And Lo! the Hunter of the East has caught
> The Sultán's Turret in a Noose of Light.
>
> Come, fill the Cup, and in the Fire of Spring
> The Winter Garment of Repentance fling:
>   The Bird of Time has but a little way
> To fly—and Lo! the Bird is on the Wing.

A Book of Verses underneath the Bough,
A Jug of Wine, a Loaf of Bread—and Thou
   Beside me singing in the Wilderness—
O, Wilderness were Paradise enow!

Some for the Glories of This World; and some
Sigh for the Prophet's Paradise to come;
   Ah, take the Cash, and let the Credit go,
Nor heed the rumble of a distant Drum.

Think, in this batter'd Caravanserai
Whose Portals are alternate Night and Day.
   How Sultán after Sultán with his Pomp
Abode his destined Hour, and went his way.

They say the Lion and the Lizard keep
The Courts where Jamshyd gloried and drank deep:
   And Bahrám, that great Hunter—the Wild Ass
Stamps o'er his Head, but cannot break his Sleep.

I sometimes think that never blows so red
The Rose as where some buried Caesar bled;
   That every Hyacinth the Garden wears
Dropt in her lap from some once lovely Head.

Ah, make the most of what we yet may spend,
Before we too into the Dust descend;
   Dust unto Dust, and under Dust to lie;
Sans Wine, sans Song, sans Singer, and—sans End!

Annabel Lee

Edgar Allan Poe

Edgar Allan Poe was born in Boston in 1809 the son of itinerant actors who died soon after. He was adopted by a long-suffering tobacco exporter of Richmond, Virginia, called John Allan whose name he incorporated in his own. He had a career of drunkenness and gambling which undid effectively a reputation for academic brilliance. He even did well at West Point, the US Military Academy, but arranged to be dismissed. By the age of thirty he had already established a reputation as a poet and later as a writer of Gothic tales and of the first modern detective fiction. He married a thirteen-year-old cousin, Virginia Clemm, in 1836 who died in 1847 not long before his headlong regimen of drink and drugs led to his own often courted death in 1849.

"Annabel Lee" is rank with necrophilia but still very appealing and published in the year of his death.

It was many and many a year ago,
    In a kingdom by the sea,
That a maiden there lived whom you may know
    By the name of Annabel Lee;—
And this maiden she lived with no other thought
    Than to love and be loved by me.

She was a child and I was a child,
    In this kingdom by the sea,
But we loved with a love that was more than love—
    I and my Annabel Lee—
With a love that the wingéd seraphs of Heaven
    Coveted her and me.

And this was the reason that, long ago,
 In the kingdom by the sea,
A wind blew out of a cloud by night
 Chilling my Annabel Lee;
So that her highborn kinsmen came
 And bore her away from me,
To shut her up in a sepulchre
 In this kingdom by the sea.

The angels, not half so happy in Heaven,
 Went envying her and me:—
Yes! that was the reason (as all men know,
 In this kingdom by the sea)
That the wind came out of the cloud, chilling
 And killing my Annabel Lee.

But our love it was stronger by far than the love
 Of those who were older than we—
 Of many far wiser than we—
And neither the angels in Heaven above
 Nor the demons down under the sea,
Can ever dissever my soul from the soul
 Of the beautiful Annabel Lee:—

For the moon never beams without bringing me dreams
 Of the beautiful Annabel Lee;
And the stars never rise but I see the bright eyes
 Of the beautiful Annabel Lee;
And so, all the night-tide, I lie down by the side
Of my darling, my darling, my life and my bride,
 In her sepulchre there by the sea—
 In her tomb by the side of the sea.

from To Helen

Edgar Allan Poe

Poe's poetry has always been more highly regarded by non-English speaking critics than at home. This one is famous if for nothing else than the nice piece of classical differentiation in the last two lines.

> Helen, thy beauty is to me
>   Like those Nicéan barks of yore,
> That gently, o'er a perfumed sea,
>   The weary, way-worn wanderer bore
>   To his own native shore.
>
> On desperate seas long wont to roam,
>   Thy Hyacinth hair, thy classic face,
> Thy Naiad airs have brought me home
>   To the glory that was Greece
>   And the grandeur that was Rome.

The Splendour Falls

Alfred Tennyson

Alfred Tennyson (he became a peer in 1884) was born in Somersby, Lincolnshire, in 1809, the son of the rector. He went to Trinity College, Cambridge, where his closest friend was Arthur Hallam. Hallam's death in 1833 had a profound effect upon him and in 1850 he published "In Memoriam," regarded as his finest work, in his friend's memory. He was buried in Poets Corner, Westminster Abbey, on 6 October 1892.
This famous lyric was based on a visit to the Killarney lakes.

The Splendour falls on castle walls
    And snowy summits old in story:
The long light shakes across the lakes,
    And the wild cataract leaps in glory.
Blow, bugle, blow set the wild echoes flying,
Blow, bugle; answer, echoes, dying dying, dying.

O hark, O hear! how thin and clear,
    And thinner, clearer, farther going!
O sweet and far from cliff and scar
    The horns of Elfland faintly blowing!
Blow, let us hear the purple glens replying:
Blow, bugle; answer, echoes, dying, dying, dying.

O love, they die in yon rich sky,
    They faint on hill or field or river;
Our echoes roll from soul to soul,
    And grow for ever and for ever.
Blow, bugle, blow set the wild echoes flying,
And answer, echoes, answer, dying, dying, dying.

from Ulysses

Alfred Tennyson

One of several classical portraits that show Tennyson's
marvellous skill in atmosphere and therapeutic nostalgia. The
"Come, my friends/Tis not too late to seek a newer world"
sequence is very often quoted by romantic young men facing the
dread prospect of marriage.

It little profits that an idle king,
By this still hearth, among these barren crags,
Match'd with an aged wife, I mete and dole
Unequal laws unto a savage race,
That hoard, and sleep, and feed, and know not me.
I cannot rest from travel: I will drink
Life to the lees: all times I have enjoy'd
Greatly, have suffer'd greatly, both with those
That loved me, and alone; on shore, and when
Thro' scudding drifts the rainy Hyades
Vext the dim sea: I am become a name;
For always roaming with a hungry heart
Much have I seen and known ; cities of men
And manners, climates, councils, governments,
Myself not least, but honour'd of them all;
And drunk delight of battle with my peers,
Far on the ringing plains of windy Troy.
I am part of all that I have met;
Yet all experience is an arch where thro'
Gleams that untravell'd world, whose margin fades
For ever and for ever when I move.
How dull it is to pause, to make an end,
To rust unburnish'd, not to shine in use!

As tho' to breathe were life. Life piled on life
Were all too little, and of one to me
Little remains: but every hour is saved
From that eternal silence, something more,
A bringer of new things; and vile it were
For some three suns to store and hoard myself,
And this gray spirit yearning in desire
To follow knowledge, like a sinking star,
Beyond the utmost bound of human thought.

* * * * *

There lies the port; the vessel puffs her sail:
There gloom the dark broad seas. My mariners,
Souls that have toil'd and wrought, and thought with me—
That ever with a frolic welcome took
The thunder and the sunshine, and opposed
Free hearts, free foreheads—you and I are old;
Old age hath yet his honour and his toil;
Death closes all: but something ere the end,
Some work of noble note, may yet be done,
Not unbecoming men that strove with Gods.
The lights begin to twinkle from the rocks:
The long day wanes: the slow moon climbs: the deep
Moans round with many voices. Come, my friends,
'Tis not too late to seek a newer world.
Push off, and sitting well in order smite
The sounding furrows; for my purpose holds
To sail beyond the sunset, and the baths
Of all the western stars, until I die.
It may be that the gulfs will wash us down:
It may be we shall touch the Happy Isles,
And see the great Achilles, whom we knew.
Tho' much is taken, much abides; and tho'
We are not now that strength which in old days
Moved earth and heaven; that which we are, we are;
One equal temper of heroic hearts,
Made weak by time and fate, but strong in will
To strive, to seek, to find, and not to yield.

from Morte D'Arthur

Alfred Tennyson

An echo of the great English epic that never was. The poem was later lengthened and included in the sequence *The Idylls of the King* completed in 1870. These pieces from beginning and end contain some of Tennyson's most famous and nostalgic lines.

> So all day long the noise of battle roll'd
> Among the mountains by the winter sea;
> Until King Arthur's table, man by man,
> Had fall'n in Lyonness about their Lord,
> King Arthur: then, because his wound was deep,
> The bold Sir Bedivere uplifted him,
> Sir Bedivere, the last of all his knights,
> And bore him to a chapel nigh the field,
> A broken chancel with a broken cross,
> That stood on a dark strait of barren land.
> On one side lay the Ocean, and on one
> Lay a great water, and the moon was full.
> Then spake King Arthur to Sir Bedivere:
> "The sequel of to-day unsolders all
> The goodliest fellowship of famous knights
> Whereof this world holds record. Such a sleep
> They sleep—the men I loved. I think that we
> Shall never more, at any future time,
> Delight our souls with talk of knightly deeds,
> Walking about the gardens and the halls
> Of Camelot, as in the days that were.
> I perish by the people which I made,—

Tho' Merlin sware that I should come again
To rule once more—but let what will be, be,

*   *   *   *   *

But now farewell, I am going a long way
With these thou seest—if indeed I go—
(For all my mind is clouded with a doubt)
To the island-valley of Avilion;
Where falls not hail, or rain, or any snow,
Nor ever wind blows loudly; but it lies
Deep-meadow'd, happy, fair with orchard-lawns
And bowery hollows crown'd with summer sea,
Where I will heal me of my grievous wound."
So said he, and the barge with oar and sail
Moved from the brink, like some full-breasted swan
That, fluting a wild carol ere her death,
Ruffles her pure cold plume, and takes the flood
With swarthy webs. Long stood Sir Bedivere
Revolving many memories, till the hull
Look'd one black dot against the verge of dawn,
And on the mere the wailing died away.

Dark Rosaleen

James Clarence Mangan

James Mangan was born in Fishamble Street in Dublin in 1803, the son of an impoverished grocer, the "Clarence" was added in maturity. He was educated by a Father Graham who taught him Latin, French, Spanish and German, in which he attained a remarkable proficiency. He worked as a scrivener's clerk for miserable wages and then he managed to live by writing for magazines. He became friendly with the clerks of the Ordinance Survey office whose work did so much to begin to establish an Irish literature in English. Work was occasionally found for him in the library in TCD. His poetry at its best is in versions of translation from other languages and though he knew no Gaelic he rendered the literal translations of O'Curry and O'Donovan into verse that still stirs. This is especially true of "Dark Rosaleen," from "Roisin Dubh" and the very witty "Bean na dTri mBo." His temperament was prone to melancholy and a little of self-dramatisation. When he wrote for *The Nation* his pseudonym was "The Man in the Cloak" (which became the title of an interesting Abbey play by Louis D'Alton). Drink, opium, an unhappy love affair finished his frail body. He died in the Meath Hospital of malnutrition in 1849.

> O, My Dark Rosaleen,
>> Do not sigh, do not weep!
> The priests are on the ocean green,
>> They march along the Deep.
> There's wine from the royal Pope,
>> Upon the ocean green;
> And Spanish ale shall give you hope,

My Dark Rosaleen!
My own Rosaleen!
Shall glad you heart, shall give you hope,
Shall give you health, and help, and hope,
My Dark Rosaleen!

Over hills, and through dales,
Have I roamed for your sake;
All yesterday I sailed with sails
On river and on lake.
The Erne, at its highest flood,
I dashed across unseen
For there was lightning in my blood,
My dark Rosaleen!
My own Rosaleen!
Oh! there was lightning in my blood,
Red lightening lightened through my blood,
My Dark Rosaleen!

All day lone, in unrest,
To and fro, do I move.
The very soul within my breast
Is wasted for you, love!
The heart in my bosom faints
To think of you, my Queen,
My life of life, my saint of saints,
My Dark Rosaleen!
My own Rosaleen!
To hear your sweet and sad complaints,
My life, my love, my saint of saints,
My Dark Rosaleen!

Woe and pain, pain and woe,
Are my lot, night and noon,
To see your bright face clouded so,
Like to the mournful moon.
But yet will I rear your throne
Again in golden sheen;
'Tis you shall reign, shall reign alone
My Dark Rosaleen!
My own Rosaleen!
'Tis you shall have the golden throne,

'Tis you shall reign, and reign alone,
    My Dark Rosaleen!

Over dews, over sands,
    Will I fly, for your weal:
Your holy, delicate white hands
    Shall girdle me with steel.
At home in our emerald bowers,
    From morning's dawn till e'en,
You'll pray for me, my flower of flowers,
    My Dark Rosaleen!
    My fond Rosaleen!
You'll think of me through daylight's hours,
My virgin flower, my flower of flowers,
    My Dark Rosaleen!

I could scale the blue air,
    I could plough the high hills,
Oh, I could kneel all night in prayer,
    To heal your many ills!
And on beamy smile from you
    Weould float like light between
My toils and me, my own, my true,
    My Dark Rosaleen!
    My fond Rosaleen!
Would give me life and soul anew,
A second life, a soul anew,
    My dark Rosaleen!

O! the Erne shall run red
    With redundance of blood,
The earth shall rock beneath our tread,
    And flames wrap hill and wood,
And gun-peal, and slogan cry
    Wake many a glen serene,
Ere you shall fade, ere you shall die,
    My Dark Rosaleen!
    My own Rosaleen!
The Judgment Hour must first be nigh,
Ere you can fade, ere you can die,
    My Dark Rosaleen!

Home-Thoughts From Abroad

Robert Browning

Robert Browning was born in London, the son of a bank clerk, in 1812. His education was informal and when he romantically married Elizabeth Browning in 1846 she was six years older than he and a much better known poet. They lived in Italy for sixteen years, mainly in Florence, where their son "Pen" was born and where Elizabeth died. Browning returned to London where his sister, Sarianna, kept house for him and lived a life, serene after all the romantic turmoil of his marriage and exile. He died in 1889 and is buried in Westminster Abbey. His reputation for "difficulty" is caused by vigorous thought and compression of style. Such lyrics as "Home-Thoughts from Abroad" are perfectly clear. He is best seen in a form known as "dramatic monologue," which he invented, and which served to compensate for the failure of some plays he attempted in his twenties. "My Last Duchess" is a brilliant and elegant horror story.

Oh, to be in England,
Now that April's there,
And whoever wakes in England
Sees, some morning, unaware,
That the lowest boughs and the brushwood sheaf
Round the elm-tree bole are in tiny leaf,
While the chaffinch sings on the orchard bough
In England—now!

And after April, when May follows,
And the white throat builds, and all the swallows—

Hark! where my blossomed pear-tree in the hedge
Leans to the field and scatters on the clover
Blossoms and dewdrops—at the bent spray's edge—
That's the wise thrush; he sings each song twice over,
Lest you should think he never could recapture
The first fine careless rapture!
And though the fields look rough with hoary dew,
All will be gay when noontide wakes anew
The buttercups, the little children's dower,
–Far brighter than this gaudy melon-flower!

My Last Duchess
Ferrara

Robert Browning

That's my last Duchess painted on the wall,
Looking as if she were alive. I call
That piece a wonder, now: Frà Pandolf's hands
Worked busily a day, and there she stands.
Will't please you sit and look at her? I said
"Frà Pandolf" by design: for never read
Strangers like you that pictured countenance,
The depth and passion of its earnest glance,
But to myself they turned (since none puts by
The curtain I have drawn for you, but I)
And seemed as they would ask me, if they durst,
How such a glance came there; so, not the first
Are you to turn and ask thus. Sir, 'twas not
Her husband's presence only, called that spot
Of joy into the Duchess' cheek: perhaps
Frà Pandolf chanced to say, "Her mantle laps
Over my lady's wrist too much," or "Paint
Must never hope to reproduce the faint
Half-flush that dies along her throat:" such stuff
Was courtesy, she thought, and cause enough
For calling up that spot of joy. She had
A heart—how shall I say? too soon made glad,
Too easily impressed; she liked whate'er
She looked on, and her looks went everywhere.
Sir, 'twas all one! My favour at her breast,
The dropping of the daylight in the West,
The bough of cherries some officious fool

Broke in the orchard for her, the white mule
She rode with round the terrace—all and each
Would draw from her alike the approving speech,
Or blush, at least. She thanked men,—good! but thanked
Somehow—I know not how—as if she ranked
My gift of a nine-hundred-years-old name
With anybody's gift. Who'd stoop to blame
This sort of trifling? Even had you skill
In speech—(which I have not)—to make your will
Quite clear to such an one, and say, "Just this
Or that in you disgusts me; here you miss,
Or there exceed the mark"—and if she let
Herself be lessoned so, nor plainly set
Her wits to yours, forsooth, and made excuse,
—E'en then would be some stooping; and I choose
Never to stoop. Oh sir, she smiled, no doubt,
Whene'er I passed her; but who passed without
Much the same smile? This grew; I gave commands;
Then all smiles stopped together. There she stands
As if alive. Will't please you rise? We'll meet
The company below, then. I repeat,
The Count your master's known munificence
Is ample warrant that no just pretence
Of mine for dowry will be disallowed;
Though his fair daughter's self, as I avowed
At starting, is my object. Nay, we'll go
Together down, sir. Notice Neptune, though,
Taming a sea-horse, thought a rarity,
Which Claus of Innsbrück cast in bronze for me?

The Owl and the Pussy Cat

Edward Lear

Edward Lear was born in Holloway, the son of a failed stockbroker, in 1812. A victim of epilepsy and asthma he was forced to earn his own living as an illustrator. He was employed by the Earl of Derby to draw the animals in his private menagerie and it was for the Earl's children he first wrote the nonsense poems for which he is famous. Nowadays his paintings and drawings are much sought after and psychologists find much to speculate about in the poems which show among other aberrations a terrible sense of loneliness. He travelled much and died in St Remo in 1888.

The Owl and the Pussy-cat went to sea
　　In a beautiful pea-green boat,
They took some honey, and plenty of money,
　　Wrapped up in a five-pound note.
The Owl looked up to the stars above,
　　And sang to a small guitar,
"O lovely Pussy! O Pussy, my love,
　　What a beautiful Pussy you are,
　　　　You are,
　　　　You are!
What a beautiful Pussy you are!"

Pussy said to the Owl, "You elegant fowl!
　　How charmingly sweet you sing!
O let us be married! too long we have tarried:
　　But what shall we do for a ring?"
They sailed away, for a year and a day,

To the land where the Bong-tree grows,
And there in a wood a Piggy-wig stood,
With a ring at the end of his nose,
His nose,
His nose,
With a ring at the end of his nose.

"Dear Pig, are you willing to sell for one shilling
Your ring?" Said the Piggy, "I will."
So they took it away, and were married next day
By the Turkey who lives on the hill.
They dined on mince, and slices of quince,
Which they ate with a runcible spoon;
And hand in hand, on the edge of the sand,
They danced by the light of the moon,
The moon,
The moon,
They danced by the light of the moon.

Lament For the Death of
Eoghan Ruadh O'Neill

Thomas Davis

Thomas Osborne Davis was born in Fermoy in 1814. A Protestant , he became a nationalist at Trinity, learned Irish and with the help of Charles Gavan Duffy's newspaper *The Nation* set out to educate the peasantry whom O'Connell had raised from their knees. It was Davis's essays on the meaning of nationhood and the songs which helped the rising people to sing about their historic and aesthetic heritage that enabled the rapid strides in nationalism to be made in the early Forties. His premature death of scarlet fever removed one of the country's most appealing leaders. He died in 1845 and is buried in Mount Jerome.

"Lament" is typical of the stirring verse and painless teaching of history that the writers of *The Nation* brought home to the renascent Irish.

Time: 10 November 1649. Scene: Ormond's Camp, Co. Waterford. Speakers: a Veteran of Eoghan O'Neill's clan, and one of the horsemen just arrived with an account of his death.

"Did they dare, did they dare, to slay Eoghan Ruadh O'Neill?"
"Yes, they slew with poison him they feared to meet with steel."
"May God wither up their hearts! May their blood cease to flow!
May they walk in living death, who poisoned Eoghan Ruadh!

"Though it break my heart to hear, say again the bitter words."
"From Derry, against Cromwell, he marched to measure swords;
But the weapons of the Saxon met him on his way,
And he died at Cloch Uachtar, upon Saint Leonard's day."

"Wail, wail ye for the Mighty One! Wail, wail ye for the Dead;
Quench the hearth, and hold the breath—with ashes strew the head.
How tenderly we loved him! How deeply we deplore!
Holy Saviour! but to think we shall never see him more!

"Sagest in the council was he, kindest in the Hall:
Sure we never won a battle—'twas Eoghan won them all.
Had he lived—had he lived—our dear country had been free;
But he's dead, but he's dead, and 'tis slaves we'll ever be.

"O'Farrell and Clanricarde, Preston and Red Hugh,
Audley and MacMahon—ye are valiant, wise, and true;
But—what, what are ye all to our darling who is gone?
The Rudder of our ship was he, our Castle's corner-stone!

"Wail, wail him through the Island! Weep, weep for our pride!
Would that on the battle-field our gallant chief had died!
Weep the Victor of Benburb—weep him, Young man and old;
Weep for him, ye woman—your Beautiful lies cold!

"We thought you would not die—we were sure you would not go,
And leave us in our utmost need to Cromwell's cruel blow—
Sheep without a shepherd, when the snow shuts out the sky—
Oh! why did you leave us, Eoghan? Why did you die?

"Soft as woman's was your voice, O'Neill! bright was your eye,
Oh! why did you leave us, Eoghan? why did you die?
Your troubles are all over, you're at rest with God on high;
But we're slaves, and we're orphans, Eoghan!— why did you die?"

Say Not the Struggle Naught Availeth

A. H. Clough

Arthur Hugh Clough was born in 1819 the son of a Liverpool cotton merchant. Conscientious and scrupulous for most of his life (he wrote to his headmaster, Arnold of Rugby, on getting a good second at Balliol, that he had failed) he was almost won over to Catholicism by Newman but elected for scepticism. He was employed at the Department of Examinations and on education business in Italy died in Florence in 1861. His death was commemorated by his friend, Matthew Arnold in the poem, "Thyrsis." "Say the struggle ..." is his most famous poem, showing not only his poetic power but also the perennial debate.

Say not the struggle naught availeth,
    The labour and the wounds are vain,
The enemy faints not, nor faileth,
    And as things have been they remain.

If hopes were dupes, fears may be liars;
    It may be, in yon smoke conceal'd,
Your comrades chase e'en now the fliers,
    And, but for you, possess the field.

For while the tired waves, vainly breaking,
    Seem here no painful inch to gain,
Far back, through creeks and inlets making,
    Come silent, flooding in, the main.

And not by eastern windows only,
    When daylight comes, comes in the light;
In front the sun climbs slow, how slowly!
    But westward, look, the land is bright!

The Last Buccaneer

Charles Kingsley

Charles Kingsley was born in Dartmoor in 1819, the son of a local vicar. He was intended for a law career but an early tendency towards the Church was seen in sermons begun at the age of four. After education at King's College, London and Magdalene College, Cambridge, he took orders in 1846, became Rector of Eversley. He was a vigorous writer of fiction and poetry, polemically anti-Catholic, and unshamedly passionate and muscular in all aspects of his life. He was a radical in politics but strongly against the Chartists threat of armed struggle. His turbulent life which included several nervous breakdowns ended comparatively early in 1875.

"The Last Buccaneer" is perhaps sentimental but in keeping with Kingsley's vigorous approach to life. "Young and Old" shows him as a poet with a flair for telling phrases which have become proverbs. It was he who first said. "Be good, sweet maid, and let who will be clever" and "... men must work and women must weep."

Oh, England is a pleasant place for them that's rich and high,
But England is a cruel place for such poor folks as I;
And such a port of mariners I ne'er shall see again,
As the peasant Isle of Avès, beside the Spanish main.

There were forty craft in Avès that were both swift and stout,
All furnished well with small arms and cannons round about;
And a thousand men in Avès made laws so fair and free
To choose their valiant captains and obey them loyally.

Thence we sailed against the Spaniard with his hoards of plate and
    gold,
Which he wrung with cruel tortures from Indian folk of old;
Likewise the merchant captains, with heart as hard as stone,
Who flog men and keel-haul them, and starve them to the bone.

Oh, the palms grew high in Avès, and fruits that shone like gold,
And the colibris and parrots they were gorgeous to behold;
And the negro maids to Avès from bondage fast did flee,
To welcome gallant sailors, a-sweeping in from sea.

Oh, sweet it was in Avès to hear the landward breeze,
A-swing with good tobacco in a net between the trees,
With a negro lass to fan you, while you listened to the roar
Of the breakers on the reef outside, that never touched the shore.

But Scripture saith, an ending to all fine things must be;
So the King's ships sailed on Avès, and quite put down were we.
All day we fought like bulldogs, but they burst the booms at night,
And I fled in a piragua, sore wounded, from the fight.

Nine days I floated starving, and a negro lass beside,
Till for all I tried to cheer her, the poor young thing she died;
But as I lay a-gasping, a Bristol sail came by,
And brought me home to England here, to beg until I die.

And now I'm old and going—I'm sure I can't tell where;
One comfort is, this world's so hard, I can't be worse off there;
If I might but be a sea-dove, I'd fly across the main,
To the pleasant Isle of Avès, to look at it once again.

Young and Old

Charles Kingsley

When all the world is young, lad,
    And all the trees are green;
And every goose a swan, lad,
    And every lass a queen;
Then hey for boot and horse, lad,
    And round the world away;
Young blood must have its course, lad,
    And every dog his day.

When all the world is old, lad,
    And all the trees are brown;
And all the sport is stale, lad,
    And all the wheels run down;
Creep home, and take your place there,
    The spent and maimed among:
God grant you find one face there,
    You loved when all was young.

Battle Hymn of the Republic

Julia Ward Howe

Julia Ward Howe was born in New York in 1819, the daughter of a banker. In 1843 she married Samuel Howe, an anti-slavery activist twenty years her senior, and became one of the Boston literati. In 1861 she visited the army of the Potomac where it was suggested to her that she write nobler words to the Federal Army's most popular march, "John Brown's Body". "The Battle Hymn of the Republic" published in 1862 in the *Atlantic Monthly* was the result. The old song by Thomas B Bishop had been and has since often been parodied down; Mrs Howe's hymn represents its only parodying up. She died in 1910.

Mine eyes have seen the glory of the coming of the Lord;
He is trampling out the vintage where the grapes of wrath are stored;
He hath loosed the fatal lightning of his terrible swift sword:
    His Truth is marching on.

I have seen him in the watch-fires of a hundred circling camps;
They have builded him an altar in the evening dews and damps;
I have read his righteous sentence by the dim and flaring lamps:
    His Day is marching on.

I have read a fiery gospel, writ in burnished rows of steel:
"As you deal with my contemners, so with you my grace shall deal;"
Let the Hero born of woman crush the serpent with his heel,
    Since God is marching on.

He had sounded forth the trumpet that shall never call retreat;
He is sifting out the hearts of men before his judgement-seat;
O be swift, my soul, to answer him; be jubilant, my feet!
  Our God is marching on.

In the beauty of the lilies Christ was born across the sea,
With a glory in his bosom that transfigures you and me;
As he died to make men holy, let us die to make men free,
  While God is marching on.

He is coming like the glory of the morning on the wave;
He is wisdom of the mighty, he is succour to the brave;
So the world shall be his footstool, and the soul of time his slave:
  Our God is marching on.

O Captain! My Captain!

Walt Whitman

Walt Whitman was born in Long Island in 1819 and received little formal education. He travelled widely and the result was *Leaves of Grass* (1855), a rhapsodic poem about America and his own burgeoning talent. He served as a nurse during the Civil War and afterwards gained a reputation for unconventionality, sexual specificity and the advocacy of total freedom. He was very much the Yankee in politics and though a Democrat, greatly admired Lincoln, whose death, which this poem celebrates, was as shocking though not so quickly disseminated as that of Kennedy nearly 100 years later. After a stroke in 1873 Whitman retired to Camden, N.J. and died there in 1892.

O Captain! my Captain! our fearful trip is done,
The ship has weather'd every rack, the prize we sought is won,
The port is near, the bells I hear, the people all exulting,
While follow eyes the steady keel, the vessel grim and daring;
    But O heart! heart! heart!
     O bleeding drops of red,
       Where on the deck my Captain lies,
        Fallen cold and dead.

O Captain! my Captain! rise up and hear the bells;
Rise up—for you the flag is flung—for you the bugle trills,
For you bouquets and ribbon'd wreaths—for you the shores
   a-crowding,
For you they call, the swaying mass, their eager faces turning;
     Here Captain! dear father!

The arm beneath your head!
   It is some dream that on the deck,
      You've fallen cold and dead.

My Captain does not answer, his lips are pale and still,
My father does not feel my arm, he has no pulse nor will,
The ship is anchor'd safe and sound, its voyage closed and done,
From fearful trip the victor ship comes in with object won;
   Exult O shores, and ring O bells!
      But I with mournful tread,
         Walk the deck my Captain lies,
            Fallen cold and dead.

Dover Beach

Matthew Arnold

Matthew Arnold was born in Middlesex in 1822 and educated in his father's school Rugby, and Balliol College, Oxford. In 1851 he was appointed Inspector of Schools, a post he held for thirty-five years, and he was responsible during that period for much educational reform. His poetry was popular and in later years he became a commentator on life as well as literature, attacking the contemporary philistinism. His work had a kind of hyper control which caused Edith Sitwell to refer to his "chilblained, mittened musing." He died in 1888.

His fears for the future of civilisation which characterise this poem seem to have been constant for it was written on his honeymoon.

> The sea is calm to-night.
> The tide is full, the moon lies fair
> Upon the straits;—on the French coast the light
> Gleams and is gone; the cliffs of England stand,
> Glimmering and vast, out in the tranquil bay.
> Come to the window, sweet is the night-air!
> Only, from the long line of spray
> Where the sea meets the moon-blanched land,
> Listen! you hear the grating roar
> Of pebbles which the waves draw back, and fling,
> At their return, up the high strand,
> Begin, and cease, and then again begin,
> With tremulous cadence slow, and bring
> The eternal note of sadness in.

Sophocles long ago
Heard it on the Aegean, and it brought
Into his mind the turbid ebb and flow
Of human misery; we
Find also in the sound a thought,
Hearing it by this distant northern sea.

The Sea of Faith
Was once, too, at the full, and round earth's shore
Lay like the folds of a bright girdle furled.
But now I only hear
Its melancholy, long, withdrawing roar,
Retreating, to the breath
Of the night-wind, down the vast edges drear
And naked shingles of the world.

Ah, love, let us be true
To one another! for the world, which seems
To lie before us like a land of dreams,
So various, so beautiful, so new,
Hath really neither joy, nor love, nor light,
Nor certitude, nor peace, nor help for pain;
And we are here as on a darkling plain
Swept with confused alarms of struggle and flight,
Where ignorant armies clash by night.

Heraclitus

William (Johnson) Cory

William Johnson Cory was born in Torrington in Devon in 1823 and educated at Eton and King's College, Cambridge. He taught at his old school for twenty-six years during which time he wrote the famous "Eton Boating Song" which was published in the school magazine in 1863. In 1872 he inherited an estate, assumed the name Cory (he had been born Johnson) and lived in Hampstead till his death in 1892. He was a skilled translator from Greek and Latin: "Heraclitus" was a version of an epigram by Callimachus the Greek poet from the 3rd century BC. The last line of the first stanza sums up the privileged pleasure of contented men.

They told me, Heraclitus, they told me you were dead;
They brought me bitter news to hear and bitter tears to shed.
I wept, as I remembered, how often you and I
Had tired the sun with talking and sent him down the sky.

And now that thou art lying, my dear old Carian guest,
A handful of grey ashes, long long ago at rest,
Still are thy pleasant voices, thy nightingales, awake;
For Death, he taketh all away, but them he cannot take.

The Fairies

William Allingham

William Allingham was born in Ballyshannon in 1824 and served as a customs officer all over Ulster. He was a shy and gentle soul, an avid apostle of Tennyson and a secret publisher of his own poetry in broadsheet. He went to live in England, joined the pre-Raphaelite Brotherhood, and become a friend of his hero, Tennyson. "The Fairies" was written when he was twenty-five at Killybegs while he was on a tour of duty. "Columbkill" crossed by the old king is Glencolmcille in south-east Donegal and the "Rosses" is Rosses Point in Co Sligo mentioned by Yeats in "The Stolen Child," whose fairies were a good deal more frightening than Allingham's. He died in 1889 and is buried in Ballyshannon.

Up the airy mountain,
    Down the rushy glen,
We daren't go a-hunting
    For fear of little men;
Wee folk, good folk,
    Trooping all together;
Green jacket, red cap,
    And white owl's feather!

Down along the rocky shore
    Some make their home,
They live on crispy pancakes
    Of yellow tide-foam;
Some in the reeds
    Of the black mountain lake,
With frogs for their watch-dogs,
    All night awake.

High on the hill-top
 The old King sits;
He is now so old and gray
 He's nigh lost his wits.
With a bridge of white mist
 Columbkill he crosses,
On his stately journeys
 From Slieveleague to Rosses;
Or going up with music
 On cold starry nights
To sup with the Queen
 Of the gay Northern Lights.

They stole little Bridget
 For seven years long;
When she came down again
 Her friends were all gone.
They took her lightly back,
 Between the night and morrow;
They thought that she was fast asleep,
 But she was dead with sorrow.
They have kept her ever since
 Deep within the lake,
On a bed of flag-leaves,
 Watching till she wake.

By the craggy hill-side,
 Through the mosses bare,
They have planted thorn-trees
 For pleasure here and there.
If any man so daring
 As dig themup in spite,
He shall find their sharpest thorns
 In his bed at night.

Up the airy mountain,
 Down the rushy glen,
We daren't go a-hunting
 For fear of little men;
Wee folk, good folk,
 Trooping all together;
Green jacket, red cap,
 And white owl's feather!

Four Ducks on a Pond

William Allingham

Allingham at his gentle and sentimental best. He was, after all, the man who turned down a lucrative offer to write a history of Ireland because he could find nothing in its story but cruelty.

Four ducks on a pond,
A grass-bank beyond,
A blue sky of spring,
White birds on the wing:
What a little thing
To remember for years—
To remember with tears!

Song

Christina Rossetti

Christina Rossetti was born in London in 1830, the younger sister of, and a better poet than, Dante Gabriel, one of the founders of the Pre-Raphaelite Brotherhood. She was a fervent Anglican, three-quarters Italian and though of great physical intensity she refused marriage twice. She stayed at home looking after an invalid mother who did not die till 1886, living the life of a lay religious. She died in 1894, one of the greatest of English women poets.

When I am dead, my dearest,
  Sing no sad songs for me;
Plant thou no roses at my head,
  Nor shady cypress tree:
Be the green grass above me
  With showers and dewdrops wet:
And if thou wilt, remember,
  And if thou wilt, forget.

I shall not see the shadows,
  I shall not feel the rain;
I shall not hear the nightingale
  Sing on as if in pain:
And dreaming through the twilight
  That doth nor rise nor set,
Haply I may remember,
  And haply may forget.

When I Set Out For Lyonnesse

Thomas Hardy

Thomas Hardy was born in Dorset, the Wessex of his novels, in 1840. He trained as an architect but in his thirties began writing a series of novels set in the West Country which increased in excellence until with *Tess of the d'Urbervilles* (1891) and *Jude the Obscure* (1895) his frankness and pessimistic view of the world caused a public outcry. He gave up the writing of fiction then to concentrate upon poetry which he regarded as superior to his prose. His verse epic on the Napoleonic Wars, *The Dynasts* was completed in 1908. He was awarded the OM in 1910 and died in 1925, having lived in happy isolation heavily protected by his second wife, Frances Dugdale. "When I set out for Lyonnesse" originated from a visit to St Juliot, Cornwall, where he went to make architectural drawings for the restoration of the church there. This was in March 1870 and he met and fell in love with Emma Gifford, the rector's sister-in-law, whom he married in 1874. "Lyonnesse" is the lost Atlantis sited between Land's End and Scilly where Tristan was born and Arthur's last great battle was fought.

> When I set out for Lyonnesse,
>   A hundred miles away,
>   The rime was on the spray,
> And starlight lit my lonesomeness
> When I set out for Lyonnesse
>   A hundred miles away.

What would bechance at Lyonnesse
  While I should sojourn there
No prophet durst declare,
  Nor did the wisest wizard guess
What would bechance at Lyonnesse
  While I should sojourn there.

When I came back from Lyonnesse
  With magic in my eyes,
All marked with mute surmise
  My radiance rare and fathomless,
When I came back from Lyonnesse
  With magic in my eyes!

The Darkling Thrush

Thomas Hardy

Hardy was not so much an atheist as a believer in malevolent
gods. In this famous poem that aridity trembles on the brink of
optimism.

I leant upon a coppice gate
  When Frost was spectre-gray,
And Winter's dregs made desolate
  The weakening eye of day.
The tangled bine-stems scored the sky
  Like strings of broken lyres,
And all mankind that haunted nigh
  Had sought their household fires.

The land's sharp features seemed to be
  The Century's corpse outleant.
His crypt the cloudy canopy,
  The wind his death-lament.
The ancient pulse of germ and birth
  Was shrunken hard and dry,
And every spirit upon earth
  Seemed fervourless as I.

At once a voice arose among
  The bleak twigs overhead
In a full-hearted evensong
  Of joy illimited;
An aged thrush, frail, gaunt, and small,
  In blast-beruffled plume,
Had chosen thus to fling his soul
  Upon the growing gloom.

So little cause for carolings
   Of such ecstatic sound
Was written on terrestrial things
   Afar or nigh around,
That I could think there trembled through
   His happy good-night air
Some blessed Hope, whereof he knew
   And I was unaware.

Spring and Fall

Gerard Manley Hopkins

Gerard Manley Hopkins was born in Stratford, Essex (now part of the metropolis) in 1844, the son of the consul for Hawaii. At Oxford he came under the influence of Newman, became a Catholic in 1866 and was ordained a Jesuit in 1877, having symbolically burned his poems but not before sending copies of them to Bridges for safe keeping. In 1884 he was appointed Professor of Classics in Newman's Catholic University of Ireland but his delicate sensibilities were unsuited to the work. He died in 1899 and was buried in Dublin, a "modern" poet before his time.

"Spring and Fall" was written when he was engaged in parish work in Liverpool in 1880—appalled by the "Vice and Horrors" from which he had been hitherto protected.

> Márgarét, are you grieving
> Over Goldengrove unleaving?
> Leáves, like the things of man, you
> With your fresh thought care for, can you?
> Ah! ás the heart grows older
> It will come to such sight colder
> By and by, nor spare a sigh
> Though worlds of wanwood leafmeal lie;
> And yet you wíll weep and know why.
> Now no matter, child, the name:
> Sórrow's spríngs áre the same.
> Nor mouth had, no nor mind, expressed
> What heart heard of, ghost guessed:
> It ís the blight man was born for,
> It is Margaret you mourn for.

Pied Beauty

Gerard Manley Hopkins

Hopkins's poetic innovations based upon stress are most clearly seen in this poem, written when he was preparing for Ordination.

Glory be to God for dappled things—
    For skies of couple-colour as a brinded cow;
        For rose-moles all in stipple upon trout that swim;
Fresh-firecoal chestnut-falls; finches' wings;
    Landscape plotted and pieced—fold, fallow, and plough;
        And, áll trádes, their gear and tackle and trim.

All things counter, original, spare, strange;
    Whatever is fickle, freckled (who knows how?)
        With swift, slow; sweet, sour; adazzle, dim;
He fathers-forth whose beauty is past change:
                    Praise him.

Duns Scotus's Oxford

Gerard Manley Hopkins

Duns Scotus was a 13th-Century Scottish Franciscan who because of his ability to make the most ingenious conceptual distinctions in concepts gave the world the word "dunce."

Towery city and branchy between towers;
Cuckoo-echoing, bell-swarmèd, lark-charmèd, rook-racked,
      river-rounded;
The dapple-eared lily below thee; that country and town did
Once encounter in, here coped and poisèd powers;

Thou hast a base and brickish skirt there, sours
That neighbour-nature thy grey beauty is grounded
Best in; graceless growth, thou hast confounded
Rural rural keeping—folk, flocks, and flowers.

Yet ah! this air I gather and I release
He lived on; these weeds and waters, these walls are what
He haunted who of all men most sways my spirits to peace;

Of realty the rarest-veinèd unraveller; a not
Rivalled insight, be rival Italy or Greece;
Who fired France for Mary without spot.

from Ode

Arthur O'Shaughnessy

Arthur William Edgar O'Shaughnessy was born in London of Irish parents in 1844. He worked as a transcriber in the British Museum and afterwards in the National History Department. He is essentially a one-poem poet but "Ode" with its selfconscious poesy and its remarkable music shows that it is better to be a one-poem poet than not one at all. He died in 1881.

We are the music makers,
    And we are the dreamers of dreams,
Wandering by lone sea-breakers,
    And sitting by desolate streams;—
World-losers and world-forsakers,
    On whom the pale moon gleams:
Yet we are the movers and shakers
    Of the world for ever, it seems.

With wonderful deathless ditties
    We build up the world's great cities,
And out of a fabulous story
    We fashion an empire's glory:
One man with a dream, at pleasure,
    Shall go forth and conquer a crown;
And three with a new song's measure
    Can trample a kingdom down.

We, in the ages lying
    In the buried past of the earth,
Built Nineveh with our sighing,
    And Babel itself in our mirth;
And o'erthrew them with prophesying
    To the old of the new world's worth;
For each age is a dream that is dying,
    Or one that is coming to birth.

Out of the Night that Covers Me

W. E. Henley

William Ernest Henley was born in Gloucester in 1848, the son of a bookseller. He lost a foot through tuberculosis and spent many painful months in hospital in treatment to save the other. This stoic poem was written at this time and there is no doubt that he was a courageous man. He became a close friend and collaborator of Robert Louis Stevenson who described him as "burly and piratical" and acknowledged him as the inspiration for "Long John Silver." He was a happy Imperialist who wrote much inspirational verse for young Britons. He died in 1903.

Out of the night that covers me,
    Black as the pit from pole to pole,
I thank whatever gods may be
    For my unconquerable soul.

In the fell clutch of circumstance
    I have not winced nor cried aloud.
Under the bludgeonings of chance
    My head is bloody, but unbow'd.

Beyond this place of wrath and tears
    Looms but the Horror of the shade,
And yet the menace of the years
    Finds, and shall find, me unafraid.

It matters not how strait the gate,
    How charged with punishments the scroll,
I am the master of my fate;
    I am the captain of my soul.

Requiem

Robert Louis Stevenson

Robert Louis Stevenson was born in Edinburgh in 1850 the son of Thomas Stevenson, a lighthouse engineer. His chronic ill-health prevented his taking up his father's strenuous profession so he studied law instead. He graduated as an advocate in 1875 but was already in love with the Bohemian ideal and, fascinated by Edinburgh lowlife determined to be a writer. He travelled much in search of health and married his wife, Fanny Osbourne, a lady ten years his senior, when her divorce came through in 1880. The success of *Treasure Island* (1883) enabled them to live in Switzerland, Bournemouth and finally in Samoa. He was an accomplished essayist, probably the most famous writer of adventure stories ever, and had a dark Calvinistic side which produced such excellent horrors as *Dr Jekyll and Mr Hyde* (1886). He died in 1894 of a brain haemorrhage at Vailima, Samoa where he is buried with this self-written epitaph.

Under the wide and starry sky,
Dig the grave and let me lie.
Glad did I live and gladly die,
    And I laid me down with a will.

This be the verse you grave for me:
Here he lies where he longed to be;
Home is the sailor, home from sea,
    And the hunter home from the hill.

from The Ballad of Reading Gaol
In Reading Goal by Reading Town

Oscar Wilde

Oscar Fingal O'Flahertie Wills Wilde was born in Dublin in 1854, the son of Sir William Wilde, the Irish surgeon and antiquary, and Jane Frances Elgee, the poet ("Speranza" of *The Nation*). A brilliant classical scholar, he went to Trinity and later Magdalen College, Oxford. He was famous as a café wit and for some of the best, epigrammatic comedy in the English theatre. He was imprisoned for homosexuality after two famous trials and after his sentence lived for three years in France. He died in Paris in 1900.

> In Reading gaol by Reading town
>   There is a pit of shame,
> And in it lies a wretched man
>   Eaten by teeth of flame,
> In a burning winding-sheet he lies,
>   And his grave has got no name.
>
> And there, till Christ call forth the dead,
>   In silence let him lie:
> No need to waste the foolish tear,
>   Or heave the windy sigh:
> The man had killed the thing he loved,
>   And so he had to die.
>
> And all men kill the thing they love,
>   By all let this be heard,
> Some do it with a bitter look,
>   Some with a flattering word,
> The coward does it with a kiss,
>   The brave man with a sword!

The Dead at Clonmacnoise

Thomas William Hazen Rolleston

Thomas William Hazen Rolleston was born in Shinrone, King's
County, in 1857. He was one of John O'Leary's circle of young men
though older than Hyde or Yeats. He helped found the Irish Literary
Society in England in 1893. He wrote much verse but apart from this
lyric his lasting claim to literary fame was his editing with Stopford
Brook of the *Treasury of Irish Verse* (1900). He died in London in 1920.

In a quiet water'd land, a land of roses,
    Stands Saint Kieran's city fair;
And the warriors of Erin in their famous generations
    Slumber there.

There beneath the dewy hillside sleep the noblest
    Of the clan of Conn,
Each below his stone with name in branching Ogham
    And the sacred knot thereon.

There they laid to rest the seven Kings of Tara,
    There the sons of Cairbré sleep—
Battle-banners of the Gael, that in Kieran's plain of crosses
    Now their final hosting keep.

And in Clonmacnoise they laid the men of Teffia,
    And right many a lord of Breagh;
Deep the sod above Clan Creidé and Clan Conaill,
    Kind in hall and fierce in fray.

Many and many a son of Conn, the Hundred-Fighter,
    In the red earth lies at rest;
Many a blue eye of Clan Colman the turf covers,
    Many a swan-white breast.

Into My Heart An Air That Kills

A.E. Housman

Alfred Edward Housman was born in 1859 in Worcester in sight of the "blue remembered hills" of Shropshire which he invested with poetic fame and half invented. He formed a strong attachment at St John's College, Oxford, with Moses Jackson who became the inspiration for his later verse. Inexplicably he did badly in his finals and he spent ten years at the patent Office. He became Professor of Latin at London University in 1892 and was appointed to the equivalent chair at Cambridge in 1911. He was the most brilliant Latinist of his time but his fame rests on a sequence of spare, beautiful poems with the title of *The Shropshire Lad* (1896). His homosexuality seems to have been almost entirely repressed. He died in 1936.

> Into my heart an air that kills
>   From yon far country blows:
> What are those blue remembered hills,
>   What spires, what farms are those?
>
> That is the land of lost content,
>   I see it shining plain,
> The happy highways where I went
>   And cannot come again.

Loveliest of Trees

A. E. Housman

The best know poem of the Shropshire sequence. It is horticulturally doubtful that Easter often saw the flowering of the cherry as far west as Shropshire.

Loveliest of trees, the cherry now
Is hung with bloom along the bough,
And stands about the woodland ride
Wearing white for Eastertide.

Now, of my threescore years and ten,
Twenty will not come again,
And take from seventy springs a score,
It only leaves me fifty more.

And since to look at things in bloom
Fifty springs are little room,
About the woodlands I will go
To see the cherry hung with snow.

In No Strange Land

"The Kingdom of God is within you."

Francis Thompson

Francis Thompson was born in Preston in 1859 and educated for
the priesthood at Ushaw College. He decided he had no vocation
but a strong religious sense prevailed in his life even when he
spent three opium-addicted years living rough in London. He
was rescued from this extremity by Alice Meynell and her
husband Wilford. Continuing addiction and tuberculosis caused
a comparatively early death but not before he had written some
memorable religious verse. He died in 1907.

> O World invisible,we view thee,
>   O world intangible, we touch thee,
> O world unknowable, we know thee,
>   Inapprehensible, we clutch thee!
>
> Does the fish soar to find the ocean,
>   The eagle plunge to find the air—
> That we ask of the stars in motion
>   If they have rumour of thee there?
>
> Not where the wheeling systems darken,
>   And our benumbed conceiving soars!—
> The drift of pinions, would we hearken,
>   Beats at our own clay-shuttered doors.
>
> The angels keep their ancient paces;—
>   Turn but a stone, and start a wing!
> 'Tis ye, 'tis your estrangéd faces,
>   That miss the many-splendoured thing.

But (when so sad thou canst not sadder)
   Cry;—and upon thy so sore loss
Shall shine the traffic of Jacob's ladder
   Pitched betwixt Heaven and Charing Cross.

Yea, in the night, my Soul, my daughter,
   Cry,—clinging Heaven by the hems;
And lo, Christ walking on the water,
   Not of Gennesareth, but Thames!

Sheep and Lambs

Katharine Tynan

Katharine Tynan was born in Clondalkin in 1861 where her father's house was a meeting place for such literary aspirants as Hyde and Yeats. She married H A Hinkson in 1883 and lived with him in Co Mayo where he was RM until his death in 1919. She wrote much poetry and more than a hundred novels but only a few of the pieces are still popular. Her phrase "pillars of the house" describing women was the title of a recent anthology of verse by women. "Sheep and Lambs" showing her slightly sentimental Catholicism is better known as a choir piece. She died in 1931.

All in the April evening,
    April airs were abroad,
The sheep with their little lambs
    Passed me by on the road.

The sheep with their little lambs
    Passed me by on the road;
All in the April evening
    I thought on the Lamb of God.

The lambs were weary, and crying
    With a weak, human cry.
I thought on the Lamb of God
    Going meekly to die.

Up in the blue, blue mountains
    Dewy pastures are sweet;
Rest for the little bodies,
    Rest for the little feet,

But for the Lamb of God,
    Up on the hilltop green,
Only a cross of shame
    Two stark crosses between.

All in the April evening,
    April airs were abroad;
I saw the sheep with their lambs,
    And thought on the Lamb of God.

Vitai Lampada

Sir Henry Newbolt

Sir Henry Newbolt, known as a weaker Kipling, has been satirised because of the confident murderous patriotism of some of his verse. He is the laureate of the smaller public school, especially his own school, Clifton, and such conceits as "playing up and playing the game" now seem spurious. Yet in his day such ideals of personal sacrifice were not considered risible. He was born in 1862, educated at Corpus Christi College, Cambridge, called to the Bar in 1887 and became chief of Telecommunications during the First World War. He was made a knight in 1915 and a CH in 1922. He died in 1938.

There's a breathless hush in the Close to-night—
    Ten to make and the match to win—
A bumping pitch and a blinding light,
    An hour to play and the last man in.
And it's not for the sake of a ribboned coat,
    Or for the selfish hope of a season's fame,
But his Captain's hand on his shoulder smote—
    "Play up! play up! and play the game!"

The sand of the desert is sodden red,—
    Red with the wreck of a square that broke;—
The Gatling's jammed and the Colonel dead,
    And the regiment blind with dust and smoke.
The river of death has brimmed his banks,
    And England's far, and Honour a name,
But the voice of a schoolboy rallies the ranks:
    "Play up! play up! and play the game!"

This is the word that year by year,
    While in her place the School is set,
Every one of her sons must hear,
    And none that hears it dare forget.
This they all with a joyful mind
    Bear through life like a torch in flame,
And falling fling to the host behind—
    "Play up! play up! and play the game!"

If

Rudyard Kipling

Joseph Rudyard Kipling was born in Bombay in 1865, the son of a sculpture teacher who afterwards became Curator of the Lahore Museum. His early life in England was very unhappy but later he enjoyed his schooldays in Devon. He became a journalist in India and was soon producing much verse and short stories. He married Caroline Starr Balestier in 1892 and lived for four years in Vermont, her home place. It was here he wrote *The Jungle Books*. He returned to England in time to celebrate the Boer War and as he saw it, responsible imperialism. He became the laureate of Empire and his verse, of a much higher quality than his detractors will admit, reached many who would otherwise have eschewed poetry. "If" is a rather daunting catalogue of traditional masculine virtues but there was a feminine side to his nature that he never denied. He wrote well for children as *Just So, Reward and Fairies* and *Stalky & Co.* clearly show. His verse is irresistible as many anti-imperialists will admit. He was the first Englishman to be awarded the Nobel prize but he refused many other decorations. He died in 1936.

> If you can keep your head when all about you
>   Are losing theirs and blaming it on you,
> If you can trust yourself when all men doubt you,
>   But make allowance for their doubting too;
> If you can wait and not be tired by waiting,
>   Or being lied about, don't deal in lies,
> Or being hated, don't give way to hating,
>   And yet don't look too good, nor talk too wise:

If you can dream—and not make dreams your master;
     If you can think—and not make thoughts your aim;
If you can meet with Triumph and Disaster
     And treat those two impostors just the same;
If you can bear to hear the truth you've spoken
     Twisted by knaves to make a trap for fools,
Or watch the things you gave your life to broken,
     And stoop and build'em up with worn-out tools:

If you can make one heap of all your winnings
     And risk it on one turn of pitch-and-toss,
And lose, and start again at your beginnings
     And never breathe a word about your loss;
If you can force your heart and nerve and sinew
     To serve your turn long after they are gone,
And so hold on when there is nothing in you
     Except the Will which says to them: "Hold on!"

If you can talk with crowds and keep your virtue,
     Or walk with Kings—nor lose the common touch,
If neither foes nor loving friends can hurt you,
     If all men count with you, but none too much;
If you can fill the unforgiving minute
     With sixty seconds' worth of distance run
Yours is the Earth and everything that's in it,
     And—which is more—you'll be a Man, my son!

Mandalay

Rudyard Kipling

"Mandalay" was written in 1890 and included in Barrack Room Ballads (1892). The Asian lover of the bluff, no-nonsense speaker and her pining seems to have had a basis in autobiographical fact.

By the old Moulmein Pagoda, lookin' eastward to the sea,
There's a Burma girl a-settin', and I know she thinks o' me;
For the wind is in the palm-trees, and the temple-bells they say:
"Come you back, you British soldier; come you back to Mandalay!"
    Come you back to Mandalay,
    Where the old Flotilla lay:
    Can't you 'ear their paddles chunkin' from Rangoon to Mandalay?
    On the road to Mandalay,
    Where the flyin'-fishes play,
    An' the dawn comes up like thunder outer China crost the Bay!

'Er petticoat was yaller an' 'er little cap was green,
An' 'er name was Supi-yaw-lat—jes' the same as Theebaw's Queen,
An' I seed her first a -smokin' of a whackin' white cheroot,
An' a-wastin' Christian kisses on an 'eathen idol's foot:
    Bloomin' idol made o' mud—
    Wot they called the Great Gawd Budd—
    Plucky lot she cared for idols when I kissed 'er where she stud!
    On the road to Mandalay ...

When the mist was on the rice-fields an' the sun was droppin' slow,
She'd git 'er little banjo an' she'd sing *"Kulla-lo-lo!"*

With 'er arm upon my shoulder an' 'er cheek agin my cheek
We useter watch the streamers an' the *hathis* pilin' teak
    Elephints a-pilin' teak
    In the sludgy, squdgy creek,
    Where the silence 'ung that 'eavy you was 'arf afraid to speak!
    On the road to Mandalay ...

But that's all shove be'ind me—long ago an' fur away,
An' there ain't no 'busses runnin' from the Bank to Mandalay;
An' I'm learnin' 'ere in London what the ten-year soldier tells:
"If you've 'eard the East a-callin', you won't never 'eed naught else."
    No! you won't 'eed nothin' else
    But them spicy garlic smells,
    An' the sunshine an' the palm-trees an' the tinkly temple-bells;
    On the road to Mandalay ...

I am sick o' wastin' leather on these grittin pavin'-stones,
An' the blasted Henglish drizzle wakes the fever in my bones;
Tho' I walks with fifty 'ousemaids outer Chelsea to the Strand,
An' they talks a lot o' lovin', but wot do they understand?
    Beefy face an' grubby 'and—
    Law! wot do they understand?
    I've a neater, sweeter maiden in a cleaner, greener land!
    On the road to Mandalay ...

Ship me somewheres east of Suez, where the best is like the worst,
Where here aren't no Ten Commandments an' a man can raise a
    thirst;
    For the temple-bells are callin', an' it's there that I would be—
    By the old Moulmein Pagoda, looking lazy at the sea;
                          Repeat Chorus

The Lake Isle of Innisfree

William Butler Yeats

William Butler Yeats, arguably the finest poet of this century, was born in Dublin in 1865, the son of John B Yeats, a famous portrait painter and nationalist. The family were intermittently poor and Yeats spent a lot of his boyhood in Sligo with the Pollexfens, his mother's people. He gave up the practice of art for literature, his early verse combining elaborate Pre-Raphaelite elegance with a new dimension found in the West of Ireland, which he called the Celtic Twilight. In the Nineties he fell in love with Maud Gonne, a beautiful, wayward republican, a love which deepened his commitment to Ireland. With the help of Lady Gregory of Coole Park he founded an Irish theatre movement and with Miss Horniman's money built the Abbey Theatre. When both Maud and her daughter Iseult rejected him he married Georgie Hyde-Lees in 1917. His wife's automatic writing gave a further spur to his mysticism and the poetry written out of this often daft vision was stronger, more declamatory and eventually great. He played an active if oblique part in politics, as a senator of the new state. He died on 28 January 1939, in Roquebrune in the south of France. After the war his remains were reburied according to his instructions in Drumcliffe Churchyard, Co. Sligo. Yeats was the most self-conscious artist possible. His egotism arose partly from shyness but became a drive which resulted in great poetry.

Yeats's poetry changed remarkably with each new aspect of his often troubled and busy life. The almost too famous "Innisfree" was written in London out of a memory of Lough Gill in Co Sligo and after a reading of Thoreau's world-forsaking *Walden.*

I will arise and go now, and go to Innisfree,
And a small cabin build there, of clay and wattles made;
Nine bean rows will I have there, a hive for the honey-bee,
And live alone in the bee-loud glade.

And I shall have some peace there, for peace comes dropping
    slow,
Dropping from the veils of the morning to where the cricket sings;
There midnight's all a-glimmer, and noon a purple glow,
And evening full of the linnet's wings.

I will arise and go now, for always night and day
I hear lake water lapping with low sounds by the shore;
While I stand on the roadway, or on the pavements gray,
I hear it in the deep heart's core.

The Second Coming

William Butler Yeats

Turning and turning in the widening gyre
The falcon cannot hear the falconer;
Things fall apart; the centre cannot hold;
Mere anarchy is loosed upon the world,
The blood-dimmed tide is loosed, and everywhere
The ceremony of innocence is drowned;
The best lack all conviction, while the worst
Are full of passionate intensity.

Surely some revelation is at hand;
Surely the Second Coming is at hand.
The Second Coming! Hardly are those words out
When a vast image our of *Spiritus Mundi*
Troubles my sight: somewhere in the sands of the desert
A shape with lion body and the head of a man,
A gaze blank and pitiless as the sun,
Is moving its slow thighs, while all about it
Reel shadows of the indignant desert birds.
The darkness drops again; but now I know
That twenty centuries of stony sleep
Were vexed to nightmare by a rocking cradle,
And what rough beast, its hour come round at last,
Slouches towards Bethlehem to be born?

Non Sum Qualis Eram Bonae Sub Regno Cynarae

Ernest Dowson

Ernest Christopher Dowson was born in Kent in 1867 and spent much of his youth and later life in France. He left his Oxford College, Queen's, without taking his degree, to work in his father's dry-dock. The "Cynara" of his most famous poem (which gave both Cole Porter and Margaret Mitchell titles for their works) was the daughter of an Italian cafe owner who afterwards married a waiter. Both his parents were tubercular and committed suicide and their son died of TB aggravated by drink. He was friendly with the Yellow Book writers and artists and like many of them became a Catholic, as much for aesthetic as for devotional reasons. He died in 1900.

> Last night, ah, yesternight, betwixt her lips and mine
> There fell thy shadow, Cynara! thy breath was shed
> Upon my soul between the kisses and the wine;
> And I was desolate and sick of an old passion.
>   Yea, I was desolate and bowed my head:
> I have been faithful to thee, Cynara! in my fashion.
>
> All night upon mine heart I felt her warm heart beat,
> Night-long within mine arms in love and sleep she lay;
> Surely the kisses of her bought red mouth were sweet;
> But I was desolate and sick of an old passion,
>   When I awoke and found the dawn was gray:
> I have been faithful to thee, Cynara! in my fashion.

I have forgot much, Cynara! gone with the wind,
Flung roses, roses riotously with the throng,
Dancing, to put thy pale, lost lilies out of mind;
But I was desolate and sick of an old passion,
   Yea, all the time, because the dance was long:
I have been faithful to thee, Cynara! in my fashion.

I cried for madder music and for stronger wine,
But when the feast is finished and the lamps expire,
Then falls they shadow, Cynara! the night is thine;
And I am desolate and sick of an old passion,
   Yea, hungry for the lips of my desire:
I have been faithful to thee, Cynara! in my fashion.

They Are Not Long
Vitae summa brevis spem nos vetat inchoare longam

Ernest Dowson

Another remarkably persistent poem with a nice *fin-de-siècle* dying fall.

> They are not long, the weeping and the laughter,
>   Love and desire and hate:
> I think they have no portion in us after
>   We pass the gate.
>
> They are not long, the days of wine and roses:
>   Out of a misty dream
> Our path emerges for awhile, then closes
>   Within a dream.

Leisure

William Henry Davies

William Henry Davies was born in Newport, Mommouth, in 1871. He went to America, worked as a fruit-picker and cattleman until he lost a foot while "jumping" a freight-car in Canada. He returned to England and supported himself by selling laces and ribbons and singing in the street. He was befriended by Bernard Shaw and Edward Thomas who lent him a cottage in Kent and enabled him to write his famous account *Autobiography of a Super-Tramp* (1907). He died in 1940.

What is this life if, full of care,
We have no time to stand and stare?

No time to stand beneath the boughs
And stare as long as sheep or cows.

No time to see, when woods we pass,
Where squirrels hide their nuts in grass.

No time to see, in broad daylight,
Streams full of stars, like skies at night.

No time to turn at Beauty's glance,
And watch her feet, how they can dance.

No time to wait till her mouth can
Enrich that smile her eyes began.

A poor life this if, full of care,
We have no time to stand and stare.

Roundabouts and Swings

Patrick Reginald Chalmers

Patrick Reginald Chalmers was born in Forfar in 1874 and educated at Rugby. He joined the banking service and combined City life with writing. *Who's Who* lists more than two dozen of his books on hunting, the countryside and poetry. I cannot discover which came first, the Chalmers poem (first printed in *Punch*) or the proverbial expression about how in life things tend to balance out. Whatever, it is a very elegant illustration (and I believe the *literary* origin) of a very useful phrase. Chalmers died in 1942.

It was early last September nigh to Framlin'am-on Sea,
An' 'twas Fair-day come to-morrow, an' the time was after tea,
An' I met a painted caravan adown a dusty lane,
A Pharoah with his wagons comin' jolt an' creak an' strain;
A cheery cove an' sunburnt, bold o' eye and wrinkled up,
An' beside him on the splashboard sat a brindled tarrier pup,
An' a lurcher wise as Solomon an' lean as fiddle-strings
Was joggin' in the dust along 'is roundabouts and swings.

"Goo'-day," said 'e; "Goo'-day," said I; "an' 'ow d'you find things go,
An' what's the chance o' millions when you runs a travellin' show?"
"I find," said 'e, "things very much as 'ow I've always found,
For mostly they goes up and down or else goes round and round."
Said 'e, "The job's the very spit o' what it always were,

It's bread and bacon mostly when the dog don't catch a 'are;
But lookin' at it broad, an' while it ain't no merchant king's,
What's lost upon the roundabouts we pulls up on the
    swings!"

"Goo' luck," said 'e; "Goo' luck," said I; "you've put it past
    a doubt;
An' keep that lurcher on the road, the gamekeepers is out;"
'E thumped upon the footboard an' 'e lumbered on again
To meet a gold-dust sunset down the owl-light in the lane;
An' the moon she climbed the 'azels, while a nightjar
    seemed to spin
That Pharaoh's wisdom o'er again, 'is sooth of lose-and-
    win;
For "up an' down an' round," said 'e, "goes all appointed
    things,
An' losses on the roundabouts means profits on the swings!"

The Donkey

G.K. Chesterton

Gilbert Keith Chesterton was born in London in 1874, the son of an estate agent. He was educated at St Paul's School and later at the Slade School of Art. He became a journalist and earned a world reputation for essays which exploited a paradoxical view of life. His verse, short stories and novels were characterised by odd humour, a firm belief in Christianity and a celebration of a Merrie England whose pre-Reformation virtues he persistently praised. His incorrigible late-Victorian and Edwardian attitudes can at times become wearisome but he is always rewarding and forgivable. He died in 1936. "The Donkey" shows him at his most characteristic—a neat versifier and a believer in God the Paradoxist.

> When fishes flew and forests walked
>   And figs grew upon thorn,
> Some moment when the moon was blood
>   Then surely I was born.
>
> With monstrous head and sickening cry
>   And ears like errant wings,
> The devil's walking parody
>   On all four-footed things.
>
> The tattered outlaw of the earth,
>   Of ancient crooked will,
> Starve, scourge, deride me: I am dumb,
>   I keep my secret still.
>
> Fools! For I also had my hour;
>   One far fierce hour and sweet:
> There was a shout about my ears,
>   And palms before my feet.

The Rolling English Road

G.K. Chesterton (1874-1936)

Chesterton the rollicking, Christian, drinking Englishman, happy at home, distrustful of foreigners, especially non-Europeans, but finding salvation in the last verse in Death the jolly inn.

Before the Roman came to Rye or out of Severn strode,
The rolling English drunkard made the rolling English road.
A reeling road, a rolling road, that rambles round the shire,
And after him the parson ran, the sexton and the squire;
A merry road, a mazy road, and such as we did tread
The night we went to Birmingham by way of Beachy Head

I know no harm of Bonaparte and plenty of the Squire,
And for to fight the Frenchman I did not much desire;
But I did bash their baggonets because they came arrayed
To straighten out the crooked road an English drunkard made,
Where you and I went down the lane with ale-mugs in our hands,
The night we went to Glastonbury by way of Goodwin Sands.

His sins they were forgiven him; or why do flowers run
Behind him; and the hedges all strengthening in the sun?
The wild thing went from left to right and knew not which was which,
But the wild rose was above him when they found him in the ditch.
God pardon us, nor harden us; we did not see so clear
The night we went to Bannockburn by way of Brighton Pier.

My friends, we will not go again or ape an ancient rage,
Or stretch the folly of our youth to be the shame of age,
But walk with clearer eyes and ears this path that wandereth;
And see undrugged in evening light the decent inn of death;
For there is good news yet to hear and fine things to be seen
Before we go to Paradise by way of Kensal Green.

Cargoes

John Masefield

John Masefield was born in Hertfordshire in 1878 and educated at Kings School, Warwick, and the training ship, *Conway*. His idyllic youth was ended by the death of his mother and the naval training which was imposed by relatives did not really suit a lad who suffered acutely from sea-sickness. He left the sea after a breakdown and after rough living in New York came home to a career as a writer. He wrote novels, poetry and autobiography and some books for children. "Cargoes" appeared in 1910 after which he did *not* go down to the sea again. He became Poet Laureate in 1930 on the death of Robert Bridges and was awarded the OM in 1935. He died in 1967, chiefly remembered for his sea-poems.

Quinquireme of Nineveh from distant Ophir
Rowing home to haven in sunny Palestine,
With a cargo of ivory,
And apes and peacocks,
Sandalwood, cedarwood, and sweet white wine.

Stately Spanish galleon coming from the Isthmus,
Dipping through the tropics by the palm-green shores,
With a cargo of diamonds,
Emeralds, amethysts,
Topazes, and cinnamon, and gold moidores.

Dirty British coaster with a salt-caked smoke stack
Butting through the Channel in the mad March days,
With a cargo of Tyne coal,
Road-rail, pig-lead,
Firewood, iron-ware, and cheap tin trays.

The Road not Taken

Robert Frost

Robert Lee Frost was born in San Francisco of New England stock in 1874 and lived most of his life in New England. He died in 1963. Though seemingly a description of a simple incident such as any country man might experience, this poem is about his art and his commitment to the life that "made all the difference."

Two roads diverged in a yellow wood,
And sorry I could not travel both
And be one traveler, long I stood
And looked down one as far as I could
To where it bent in the undergrowth;

Then took the other, as just as fair,
And having perhaps the better claim,
Because it was grassy and wanted wear;
Though as for that the passing there
Had worn them really about the same,

And both that morning equally lay
In leaves no step had trodden black.
Oh, I kept the first for another day!
Yet knowing how way leads on to way,
I doubted if I should ever come back.

I shall be telling this with a sigh
Somewhere ages and ages hence:
Two roads diverged in a wood, and I—
I took the one less traveled by,
And that has made all the difference.

John-John

Thomas MacDonagh

Thomas MacDonagh was born in Cloughjordan, Co. Tipperary, in 1878. He met Padraic Pearse in Aran in 1908 and agreed to collaborate in the St Enda's venture. When the school was opened in Ranelagh that September he was the first teacher. He joined the English Department of UCD in 1912 and in 1914 became director of training for the Irish Volunteers. He joined the Military Council of the IRB in 1915 and was one of the chief planners of the Easter Rising, a signatory of the Proclamation of the Republic and commander of the insurgents in Jacob's. He was executed on May 3 with Pearse and Clarke. He wrote much poetry and was one of the founders, with Martyn and Plunkett, of the Irish Theatre in Hardwick Street in 1914. "John-John" is a beautiful if not very realistic love poem.

I dreamt last night of you, John-John,
    And thought you called to me;
And when I woke this morning, John,
    Yourself I hoped to see;
But I was all alone, John-John,
    Though still I heard your call:
I put my boots and bonnet on,
    And took my Sunday shawl,
    And went, full sure to find you, John,
                    To Nenagh fair.

The fair was just the same as then,
    Five years ago to-day,
When first you left the thimble men
    And came with me away;
For there again were thimble men
    And shooting galleries,
And card-trick men and Maggie men
    Of all sorts and degrees—
But not a sight of you, John-John,
                Was anywhere.

I turned my face to home again,
    And called myself a fool
To think you'd leave the thimble men
    And live again by rule,
And go to Mass and keep the fast
    And till the little patch:
My wish to have you home was past
    Before I raised the latch
And pushed the door and saw you, John,
                Sitting down here.

How cool you came in here, begad,
    As if you owned the place!
But rest yourself there now, my lad,
    'Tis good to see your face;
My dream is out, and now by it
    I think I know my mind:
At six o'clock this house you'll quit,
    And leave no grief behind;—
But until six o'clock, John-John,
                My bit you'll share

The neighbours' shame of me began
    When first I brought you in
To wed and keep a tinker man
    They thought a kind of sin;
But now this three year since you're gone
    'Tis pity me they do,

And that I'd rather have, John-John,
 Than that they'd pity you.
Pity for me and you, John-John,
     I could not bear.

Oh, you're my husband right enough,
 But what's the good of that?
You know you never were the stuff
 To be the cottage cat,
To watch the fire and hear me lock
 The door and put out Shep—
But there now, it is six o'clock
 And time for you to step.
God bless and keep you far, John-John!
    And that's my prayer.

Adlestrop

Edward Thomas

Philip Edward Thomas was born in London in 1878 and educated at St Paul's School and Lincoln College, Oxford. He married while still an undergraduate and he and his wife, Helen Noble, lived in near poverty while he tried to earn a living by hack writing. He joined the army in 1915 as a private but by the time he was killed at Arras in 1917 he had been commissioned. He is now much more highly thought of than his contemporaries. "Adlestrop" is the kind of perfect topographical poem that made readers think he was one of the Georgians.

Yes. I remember Adlestrop—
The name, because one afternoon
Of heat the express-train drew up there
Unwontedly. It was June.

The steam hissed. Some one cleared his throat.
No one left and no one came
On the bare platform. What I saw
Was Adlestrop—only the name

And willows, willow-herb, and grass,
And meadowsweet, and haycocks dry,
No whit less still and lonely fair
Than the high cloudlets in the sky.

And for that minute a blackbird sang
Close by, and round him mistier,
Farther and farther, all the birds
Of Oxfordshire and Gloucestershire.

The Wayfarer

Padraic Pearse

Patrick Henry Pearse was born in Dublin in 1879, the son of an English father and an Irish mother. He was educated at the CBS in Westland Row and graduated from the Royal University as a barrister but he rarely practised. His ideal of a free and Gaelic Ireland led to the founding of a school, St Enda's, which followed his own carefully thought-out ideas of education. He became the first president of the Provisional Irish Republic promulgated on the steps of the GPO, Dublin, on Easter Monday, 1916. He was among the first batch of insurgents to be shot, on May 3 1916. "The Wayfarer" was written in Kilmainham Jail on May 2. Its evocation of an ideal Ireland is practically a Last Will and Testament.

> This beauty of the world hath made me sad,
> This beauty that will pass;
> Sometimes my heart hath shaken with great joy
> To see a leaping squirrel in a tree,
> Or a red lady-bird upon a stalk,
> Or little rabbits in a field at evening,
> Lit by a slanting sun,
> Or some green hill where shadows drifted by,
> Some quiet hill where mountainy man hath sown
> And soon will reap, near to the gate of Heaven;
> Or children with bare feet upon the sands
> Of some ebbed sea, or playing on the streets
> Of little towns in Connacht,
> Things young and happy.
> And then my heart hath told me:
> These will pass,
> Will pass and change, will die and be no more,
> Things bright and green, things young and happy;
> And I have gone upon my way
> Sorrowful.

A Piper

Seumas O'Sullivan

Seumas O'Sullivan was born James Sullivan Starkey in Rathmines in 1879. He was a friend of Yeats and AE and an influential figure in the Literary Revival, both as poet and literary adviser. He founded *The Dublin Magazine* in 1923 and for thirty years it was an important element in the country's cultural life. He died in 1958. "A Piper" is one of a series of street poems of Dublin city's life which has broken through the skin of "poetry" to become part of the life of the Plain People of Ireland.

A Piper in the street today,
Set up, and tuned, and started to play,
And away, away, away on the tide
Of his music we started; on every side
Doors and windows were opened wide,
And men left down their work and came,
And women with petticoats coloured like flame,
And little bare feet that were blue with cold,
Went dancing back to the age of gold,
And all the world went gay, went gay,
For half an hour in the street today.

November Skies

John Freeman

John Freeman was born in Middlesex in 1880, the son of a commercial traveller. He left school at the age of twelve to become the office boy in an insurance firm of which he had become director before he died in 1929. He wrote much poetry and several critical works, notably on George Moore and Melville. In spite of its "soft" Georgian subject this much-anthologised piece shows close and idiosyncratic observation.

Than these November skies
Is no sky lovelier. The clouds are deep;
Into their grey the subtle spies
Of colour creep,
Changing that high austerity to delight,
Till ev'n the leaden interfolds are bright.
And, where the cloud breaks, faint far azure peers
Ere a thin flushing cloud again
Shuts up that loveliness, or shares.
The huge great clouds move slowly, gently, as
Reluctant the quick sun should shine in vain,
Holding in bright caprice their rain.
        And when of colours none,
Nor rose, nor amber, nor the scarce late green
Is truly seen,—
In all the myriad grey,
In silver height and dusky deep, remain
The loveliest,
Faint purple flushed of the unvanquished sun.

A Ship, An Isle, A Sickle Moon

James Elroy Flecker

James Elroy Flecker was born in Lewisham in 1884 and educated at Oxford and Cambridge where he studied Oriental Languages as a preparation for the Consular Service. In 1910 he was posted to Constantinople where he married a Greek girl, Hella Skiardessi. From 1911 until his health broke in early 1913 he was Vice-Consul in Beirut (a more popular posting then than now) and he died in a sanatorium in Davos in 1915. His preoccupation with the Middle East began when he stole his first copy of Fitzgerald's *Rubaiyat*. His most famous work is the play *Hassan* which had a spectacular production in 1922 with choreography by Fokine and music by Delius.

A ship, an isle, a sickle moon—
With few but with how splendid stars
The mirrors of the sea are strewn
Between their silver bars!

An isle beside an isle she lay,
The pale ship anchored in the bay,
While in the young moon's port of gold
A star-ship—as the mirrors told—
Put forth its great and lonely light
To the unreflecting Ocean, Night.
And still, a ship upon her seas,
The isle and the island cypresses
Went sailing on without the gale:
And still there moved the moon so pale,
A cresent ship without a sail!

Wander-Thirst

Gerald Gould

Gerald Gould was born in Scarborough in 1885 and was a fellow of Merton College from 1909 to 1916. Afterwards he pursued a career of literary journalism until his death in 1936. "Wander-Thirst" is a typical poem of an unadventurous age. Go he didn't! Yet it does touch a nerve in many who wished they could.

Beyond the East the sunrise, beyond the West the sea,
And East and West the wander-thirst that will not let me be;
For the seas call and the stars call, and oh! the call of the sky.

I know not where the white road runs, nor what the blue hills are,
But a man can have the Sun for friend, and for his guide a star;
And there's no end of voyaging when once the voice is heard,
For the river calls and the road calls, and oh! the call of a bird!

Yonder the long horizon lies, and there by night and day
The old ships draw to home again, the young ships sail away;
And come I may, but go I must, and, if men ask you why,
You may put the blame on the stars and the Sun and the white
    road and the sky.

The Soldier

Rupert Brooke

Rupert Chawner Brooke was born in 1887 at Rugby School where his father was a housemaster and educated there and at King's College, Cambridge. His charm, physical beauty, anticipatory patriotic poems and early death made him the archetypical English youth dying for a great cause. He was not in fact so naive. He died of septicaemia on a hospital ship in the Aegaean in 1915.

If I should die, think only this of me:
    That there's some corner of foreign field
That is for ever England. There shall be
    In that rich earth a richer dust concealed;
A dust whom England bore, shaped, made aware,
    Gave, once, her flowers to love, her ways to roam,
A body of England's, breathing English air,
    Washed by the rivers, blest by suns of home.

And think, this heart, all evil shed away,
    A pulse in the eternal mind, no less
        Gives somewhere back the thoughts by England given;
Her sights and sounds; dreams happy as her day;
And laughter, learnt of friends; and gentleness,
    In heart at peace, under an English heaven.

Lament for the Poets: 1916

Francis Ledwidge

Francis Ledwidge was born in Slane, Co Meath, in 1887 the son of an
evicted tenant. Lord Dunsany, the local landlord, encouraged him to
write and to join the army at the outbreak of war in 1914. He survived
the Gallipoli landing but was killed in Belgium in 1917. He was
stationed at Ebrington Barracks in Derry when word came of the Easter
Rising.

I heard the Poor Old Woman say:
"At break of day the fowler came,
And took my blackbirds from their songs
Who loved me well thro' shame and blame.

"No more from lovely distances
Their songs shall bless me mile by mile
Nor to white Ashbourne call me down
To wear my crown another while.

"With bended flowers the angels mark
For the skylark the place they lie,
From there its little family
Shall dip their wings first in the sky.

"And when the first surprise of flight
Sweet songs excite, from the far dawn
Shall there come blackbirds loud with love,
Sweet echoes of the singers gone.

"But in the lonely hush of eve
Weeping I grieve the silent bills."
I heard the Poor Old Woman say
In Derry of the little hills.

Rendezvous

Alan Seeger

Alan Seeger was born in New York in 1888 at educated at Harvard where he edited the *Harvard Monthly*. He joined the French Foreign Legion and was awarded the Médaille Militaire and the Croix de Guerre before being killed at Belloy-en-Santerre in 1917.

> I have a rendezvous with Death
> At some disputed barricade,
> When Spring comes back with rustling shade
> And apple-blossoms fill the air—
> I have a rendezvous with Death
> When Spring brings back blue days and fair.
>
> It may be he shall take my hand
> And lead me into his dark land
> And close my eyes and quench my breath—
> It may be I shall pass him still.
> I have a rendezvous with Death
> On some scarred slope of battered hill.
> When Spring comes round again this year
> And the first meadow-flowers appear.
>
> God knows 'twere better to be deep
> Pillowed in silk and scented down,
> Where love throbs out in blissful sleep,
> Pulse nigh to pulse, and breath to breath.
> Where hushed awakenings are dear ...
> But I've a rendezvous with Death
> At midnight in some flaming town,
> When Spring trips north again this year,
> And I to my pledged word am true,
> I shall not fail that rendezvous.

The Planter's Daughter

Austin Clarke

Austin Clarke was born in Dublin in 1896 and lived for most of his boyhood near the Black Church which dominated his childhood imagination and gave him the title of his autobiography, *Twice Round the Black Church*. He was a poet of rich colour and vigorous language, strongly influenced by Gaelic which he had been taught by Hyde at UCD. He also wrote poetic plays and founded a society to speak the lines properly. He died in 1974.

When night stirred at sea
And the fire brought a crowd in,
They say that her beauty
Was music in mouth
And few in the candlelight
Thought her too proud,
For the house of the planter
Is known by the trees.

Men that had seen her
Drank deep and were silent,
The women were speaking
Wherever she went—
As a bell that is rung
Or a wonder told shyly,
And O she was the Sunday
In every week.

Not Waving but Drowning

Stevie Smith

Stevie Smith was christened Florence Margaret in Hull in 1902 but lived most of her adult life in North London with an aunt. She wrote three novels but is best know for her verse which she read well and often illustrated by comic drawings. This, her most famous poem, was first published in *Punch*. She died in 1971.

Nobody heard him, the dead man,
But still he lay moaning:
I was much further out than you thought
And not waving but drowning.

Poor chap, he always loved larking
And now he's dead
It must have been too cold for him his heart gave way,
They said.

Oh, no no no, it was too cold always
(Still the dead one lay moaning)
I was much too far out all my life
And not waving but drowning.

Shancoduff

Patrick Kavanagh

Patrick Kavanagh was born in Monaghan in 1906 and lived there as farmer, cobbler and writer until his move to Dublin in 1919. He had already made a name for himself as poet and prose-writer with *Ploughman* (1936) and *The Green Fool* (1938). With *The Great Hunger* (1942) he earned the mixture of fame and abuse that was a feature of literary life in the Ireland at the time. His largely autobiographical novel *Tarry Flynn* confirmed his reputation as a writer, while his prickly, litigious nature gradually mellowed. He died in 1967, regarded as one of Ireland's finest poets. "Shancoduff" is a Monaghan poem based on the rich, tough and stifling life of the rural Ireland of the Thirties. "On Raglan Road" describes an epiphany from his Dublin period.

> My black hills have never seen the sun rising
> Eternally they look north towards Armagh
> Lot's wife would not be salt if she had been
> Incurious as my black hills that are happy
> When dawn whitens Glassdrummond chapel.
>
> My hills hoard the bright shillings of March
> While the sun searches in every pocket.
> They are my Alps and I have climbed the Matterhorn
> With a sheaf of hay for three perishing calves
> In the field under the Big Forth of Rocksavage.
>
> The sleety winds fondle the rushy beards of Shancoduff
> While the cattle-drovers sheltering in the Featherna Bush
> Look up and say: "Who owns them hungry hills
> That the water-hen and snipe must have forsaken?
> A poet? Then by heavens he must be poor."
> I hear and is my heart not badly shaken?

On Raglan Road

Patrick Kavanagh

On Raglan Road on an autumn day I met her first and knew
That her dark hair would weave a snare that I might one day rue;
I saw the danger, yet I walked along the enchanted way,
And I said, let grief be a fallen leaf at the dawning of the day.

On Grafton Street in November we tripped lightly along the ledge
Of the deep ravine where can be seen the worth of passion's
    pledge,
The Queen of Hearts still making tarts and I not making hay—
O I loved too much and by such by such is happiness thrown away.

I gave her gifts of the mind I gave her the secret sign that's known
To the artists who have known the true gods of sound and stone
And word and tint. I did not stint for I gave her poems to say.
With her own name there and her own dark hair like clouds over
    fields of May.

On a quiet street where old ghosts meet I see her walking now
Away from me so hurriedly my reason must allow
That I had wooed not as I should a creature made of clay—
When the angel wooes the clay he'd lose his wings at the dawn
    of day.

Index of Poets and Poems

POOLBEG

MY NATIVE LAND
A CELEBRATION OF BRITAIN

Edited by Sean McMahon

My Native Land is a choice gathering of well-loved poems and songs, culled from the great treasure house of British verse. It embraces the strands of many traditions, from Shakespeare to Kipling, Burns to Betjeman. It brims over with the outpourings of passionate shepherds, the rousing choruses of marching troops, the sentimental songs of the music hall. Patriotic lyrics vie with eloquent homilies; sea shanties jostle with ballads of love; nonsense verse, parodies and rhyming jingles join in the revelry. Pieces are gathered from a region extending from the glory of the English garden to the land of the Leal. This anthology is a splendid celebration of a rich and noble heritage.

POOLBEG

Rich and Rare

Edited by Sean McMahon

A treasure-house of tradition, a store of ballads, songs sung at firesides, poems recalling a noble past.

A rich vein of fantasy, humour and romance, capturing the soul of a nation.

A book for everyone who loves Ireland.

POOLBEG

———————

THE POOLBEG BOOK OF
CHILDREN'S
VERSE

Edited by Sean McMahon

For the young (and everybody else) here is a
sparkling new miscellany of poems. Into the
circus ring parades a menagerie of mystery cats,
dabbling ducks, mad dogs and weeping walruses.
Witches and vagabonds, cowboys and
highwaymen stalk the pages. There are rhymes to
dazzle, lines to ponder, magic tales to stir the
heart. A captivating blend of humour, fantasy
and legend makes this a delightful carousel of
verse.

———————

POOLBEG

Fair City

A Thousand Years of Dublin

Edited by Sean McMahon

The wit and wisdom of Dublin is celebrated in
this captivating treasury of story and verse.
Balladeers, raconteurs and biographers are here
assembled to bring the reader on a lively tour of
the fair city down through the centuries. Famous
landmarks and historical characters are brought
to life in this literary pageant. It is a delightful
gathering of facinating lore, to be savoured by
visitors as well as Dubliners.
